Waters of Wealth

Waters of Wealth

The Story of the Kootenai River

and

Libby Dam

By

Donald E. Spritzer

PRUETT **P**UBLISHING COMPANY
Boulder, Colorado 80301

© 1979 by Donald E. Spritzer
All rights reserved, including those to reproduce this book, or parts thereof, in any form without permission in writing from the Publisher.

Library of Congress Cataloging in Publication Data

Spritzer, Donald E   1946-
   Waters of wealth.

   Bibliography: p.
   Includes index.
   1. Kootenai River—History.   2. Libby Dam, Mont.   I. Title.
F1089.K7S68   971.1'45   79-9790
ISBN 0-87108-528-3 hard
ISBN 0-87108-542-9 paper

First Edition
1 2 3 4 5 6 7 8 9

Printed in the United States of America

Contents

Introduction	1
Flatbows and Horse Indians	6
The Great Land Geographer	23
Mountaineers and Missionaries	32
Wild Horse	45
The Second Mining Boom	55
The Age of Steam	79
Timber	103
The Modern Era	118
Libby Dam	136
Sources	155
Index	161

Acknowledgements

The author wishes to express appreciation to the following people: Mr. Bradley O. Luton Jr. and Mr. John Davidson of the U.S. Army Corps of Engineers for their assistance in procuring and printing photographs and handling numerous other details involved in publication; Mrs. Inez Herrig, Librarian at Libby's Lincoln County Free Library for furnishing and identifying photographs, and sending the manuscript to others for their comments; Mrs. Harriet Meloy, Brian Cockhill, and Lory Morrow of the Montana State Historical Society Library for their help with research materials and photographs; the staff of the Missoula City-County Library for help with published sources; Dr. Dale Johnson of the University of Montana Archives for photographs; Mr. W. E. Ireland of the British Columbia Provincial Library and Archives for photographs of Canada's Kootenai country; and Mr. Dan McDonald of Moyie, British Columbia and Mr. David Kay of Cranbrook, British Columbia for their comments on the manuscript. Finally, special thanks to my wife, Kathy, for typing and assistance in editing.

To Kathy, Mark and Greg

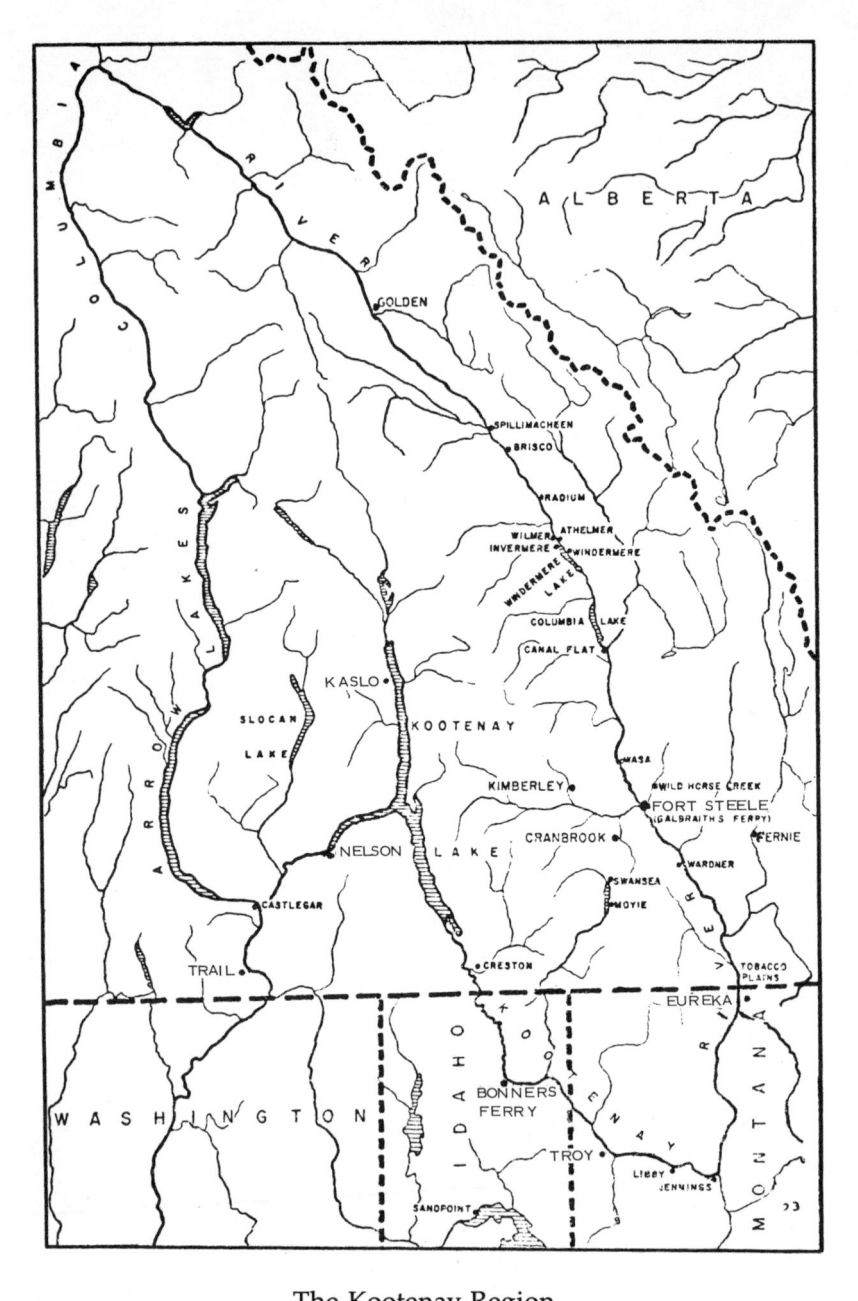

The Kootenay Region
From Hacking, Norman, "Steamboat Days on the Upper Columbia and Upper Kootenay," *British Columbia Historical Quarterly*, Vol. XVI, Jan., 1952, — *Courtesy Provincial Archives, British Columbia.*

Introduction

The history of a river is largely a tale of the men and women who have occupied its shores. Most of the Kootenai River story is a narrative of red, yellow, and white people who have lived, planned, built, and died in one of the most beautiful regions in all of North America. But the Kootenai River itself existed long before the relatively short era that man has inhabited the valley. The river is as ancient as the towering peaks which surround its six hundred mile course. These mountains had their beginnings more than one-half billion years before the advent of recorded history.

During the geological era known as the Precambrian, which ended more than five hundred million years ago, much of the area of the present Rocky Mountains slowly sank to form a long, shallow, sea-filled basin. Since there were no trees or other plants during the period to slow down erosion, material rapidly washed into this trough. Sediment nearly eight miles thick accumulated in the part of the sea which later became the Kootenai Valley. Eventually, this material became compressed into the sedimentary rock which today composes much of the Rocky, Purcell, and Cabinet Ranges surrounding the Kootenai River.*

For more than four hundred million years, the ocean waters receded and returned to the area several times, and on each

---

*One author has counted over sixty spellings of the word "Kootenai." Americans have traditionally written it as "Kootenai" while the Canadians prefer "Kootenay." Except when quoting from Canadian sources, this study will use the American spelling for the river; the Canadian spelling will be used to designate Canadian companies and Kootenay Lake.

occasion, more layers of sediment and marine fossils accumulated. During one of the periods when the seas had withdrawn, about one hundred and fifty million years ago, numerous swamps formed, and huge dinosaurs roamed the region. Very few of their remains have been found in the Kootenai country, however. The final great marine inundation of the Rocky Mountain area stretched from the Arctic to the Gulf of Mexico and covered more than one-half of North America before it receded near the end of the Cretaceous period, some seventy million years ago.

As this sea disappeared, the uplifting of the great Continental Divide began. Tremendous forces near the Earth's surface pressed inward from the area west of the present Rocky Mountains, causing the Earth's crust to fold. Older layers of rocks pushed above newer layers along giant fault lines. The result was the first Rocky Mountain chain, which took over ten million years to form. It took the rivers and streams a much shorter time to erode these mountains to a nearly flat plain. The second or present Rockies arose from block faulting forces which uplifted the land in a nearly vertical direction. The mountains grew in a series of slow but steady upward jerks which took place over thousands of years.

As a result of mountain building, large valleys developed between ridges. Two such valleys were the Rocky Mountain Trench and the Purcell Trench. The Kootenai River soon began to flow through these gorges, and the resulting erosion widened and deepened the valleys. The birth of the river occurred simultaneously with the formation of the valley, approximately twenty-five million years ago. Often mountain building took place more rapidly than river erosion and caused the ponding of many streams which eventually formed large valley lakes. On the Kootenai, lakes formed on the Tobacco Plains and near Libby and Troy, Montana. The river then wore deep gorges between the lakes, such as the present canyon between Libby and Troy, and the lakes drained. Kootenay Lake in British Columbia is the only remaining valley lake on the Kootenai.

Besides flowing water, another force helped shape the topography of the Kootenai country. Over one million years ago, with the advent of the Pleistocene period, the first of four great ice ages began. During each of these periods, huge masses of ice advanced southward from Canada, only to recede again. The last ice sheet to cover much of North America disappeared about fifteen thousand years ago. The glaciers formed as a result of cooler temperatures and high snowfall. The accumulating snow compressed into huge masses of ice which became mobile and slowly flowed down the valleys of the Rocky Mountains.

In the Kootenai region, the Cordilleran ice sheet moved southward from British Columbia. The ice traveled along the Rocky Mountain and Purcell Trenches and the Yaak and Moyie

Kootenai Falls between Libby and Troy, Montana — *Courtesy Lincoln County Library, Libby, Montana.*

valleys. The sheets were from six thousand to seven thousand feet thick and thus covered the entire area except for the tops of a few high peaks. The receding glaciers left in their wake broadened and deepened valleys and high cirques which now enclose beautiful mountain lakes. The glaciers also plowed up huge piles of debris in the form of silt, clay, and gravel.

As the last ice sheet retreated up the Kootenai, its melt water formed a huge lake which covered nearly the entire valley. Glacial Lake Kootenai probably extended as far south as Glacial Lake Missoula in Montana's Clark Fork Valley. The lake left the vast deposits of sand and silt which now border much of the river and give it its characteristic green color.

During the years since the last great ice age, the Kootenai River has been cutting through these glacial and lake deposits. In eroding down to its present bed, the river in places has left a series of terraces which are high above its present course. As the climate warmed, vegetation reappeared in the form of the pine, spruce, and fir forests which now cover much of the valley.

Today, as it winds through two nations, the Kootenai River flows across some of the most spectacular country in the Rocky Mountain West. Aside from its scenic grandeur, the Kootenai region has proven to be a fabulous source of wealth to those who have settled there, from the earliest Indians to its present inhabitants.

Throughout the relatively short period that men have lived in the area, they have exploited each of its riches in turn. To the Kutenai Indians, the river provided the main avenue of transportation linking their bands, which were scattered throughout the valley. From the waters of the Kootenai and its tributaries came the fish which composed a large part of the tribal diet. From the valleys carved by the river came the wild animals which provided food, clothing, and shelter. The Indians shaped their tools from the rocks and minerals along the river's shores.

The first white explorers to travel the river came in search of furs, mainly beaver, which were made into hats for the gentlemen of London. Later settlers came seeking mineral wealth exposed by the flowing water or hidden in nearby hills. Steamboats plying the river helped haul the first ore from the mines to the smelters. Many who failed to find their fortune in the hills remained to farm the lush topsoil deposited by the Kootenai.

The river and its tributaries also watered some of the richest forests in North America, and men eventually exploited this

Yarnell Island on Lake Koocanusa above Libby Dam — *Courtesy Lincoln County Library, Libby, Montana.*

timber wealth. The Kootenai itself served as a ready avenue to convey the logs from the forests to the first sawmills.

Finally, when men needed energy to run the mines and mills and to light the towns of the valley, they turned to the river. Huge dams and generating plants harnessed its rushing waters. Libby Dam is simply the latest attempt by man to utilize the wealth of the Kootenai River.

1

Flat Bows and Horse Indians

Thousands of years before the birth of Christ, the first men came to North America from the Eastern Hemisphere — probably across a land bridge now occupied by the Bering Straits — and scattered in all directions. Excavations in eastern Washington near the Kootenai country show that men lived in this area nearly 15,000 years ago. It was not until later that the first known residents inhabited the valley of the Kootenai. Recent studies have uncovered evidence that people who possibly came from east of the Rockies occupied the valley around 500 A.D.

The present Kutenai tribe has no legends that suggest that men lived in their area before them. When they moved into the region west of the Rockies, the Kutenais forcefully removed a small, primitive band known as the Snare Indians who resided in the mountains near the northern bow of the Columbia River. The Kutenai Indians have no remote idea regarding their place of origin. Tribal members have long maintained that they have always occupied their present domain. Evidence suggests that they have been there for nearly three hundred years.

Most likely the tribe, forced westward by more powerful enemies, migrated into the mountains from the Great Plains. They may have moved in from the north through the Rocky Mountain Trench. In any case, they spread gradually throughout the lands drained by the Kootenai and the upper reaches of the Columbia as far north as Arrow and Slocan Lakes.

Originally, the entire tribe inhabited a single small area at Tobacco Plains on the Kootenai River's eastern branch near the present American-Canadian border. Population pressure led groups to leave the region one by one to establish new settlements. The first band to migrate moved northeast to settle near present Fernie, British Columbia. Later groups moved to the regions of Libby and Jennings, Montana; Bonners Ferry, Idaho; and Fort Steele, Creston, and Windermere, British Columbia. From the time of the earliest settlers, whites have divided the Kutenai into two groups — the Upper Kutenai or Horse Indians, and the Lower Kutenai or Flat Bows, so named because their

Kootenai Indians and tepees near Cranbrook, British Columbia —
Courtesy University of Montana Library Archives.

members made straight, flat wooden bows. The Flat Bows located their first village near modern-day Bonners Ferry. From there, bands migrated and established villages on the shores of Kootenay Lake.

As the Kutenai bands dispersed, contrasting dialects and habits developed, but the tribe maintained a deep sense of unity. The main thread which tied all of the bands together, both geographically and emotionally, was the Kootenai River. It was the only physical link between villages, enabling the groups to maintain contact with each other. The Kutenai Indians knew that the river and all the land it drained was their domain, and they jealously guarded it, especially against marauding Blackfeet from the east.

The meaning of the name "Kutenai" is as obscure as are the tribe's regional origins. Most of the Kutenai informants of Montana anthropologist H. H. Turney-High agreed that the word was of Blackfeet origin and may have been applied to the tribe in a derogatory sense. In speaking of themselves, Kutenai more often have used the word "Sanka" which is said to mean "standing up straight" like an arrow in the ground. Many historians have translated "Kutenai" from the Athabascan words "coo," meaning water, and "Tinneh," meaning people, to derive "people of the lakes."

The Kutenai language is distinct from that of any known tribe in North America. The first whites who came into contact with them described their language as musical in quality and virtually unpronounceable by Europeans. The Kutenai communicated with other tribes by means of sign language. They made no attempt at writing except for the pictographs they made on cliffs and on the walls of caves. Their paint came from crushed stone and fish oil. They passed down their rich tribal folklore by word of mouth.

Despite this linguistic uniqueness, the Kutenai shared many common traits with the neighboring Salish-speaking tribes. Occasionally they joined the Flatheads and Pend D'Orielles on the always dangerous bison hunts into the Blackfeet territory east of the Rockies. Since the Upper Kutenai bands depended upon the bison for much of their food, shelter, and clothing, they invaded the land of their ancient enemies three times each year to hunt. The main bison expedition occurred in July, and smaller hunts took place in the early autumn and in mid-winter.

Before the tribe obtained horses, hunters either attempted to surround the herds and separate out weaker animals or drove them over cliffs. Once they acquired horses, hunting parties could travel more than thirty miles each day. Constant danger of enemy attack forced them to travel in a compact, military formation. They posted guards around the camp at all times. During the winter hunts they crossed the mountains on snowshoes and attempted to drive the animals into snowdrifts. They then packed the meat out in relays, each man carrying a load for about two miles.

A single Indian would not kill more than three animals in a day because he could not skin and clean more than that with his stone knife. Hunting expeditions were community projects. At camp, the women tanned the hides and prepared the meat for storage. The Kutenai seldom smoked the meat. They preferred to cut it into long strips and dry it on racks built over a fire.

The hunter's chief tool was his bow, which the Kutenai made from cedar or cherry wood. After soaking and seasoning the wood, he wrapped it in wet sinew and sometimes decorated it with snakeskin. The bowstrings, which seldom broke, consisted of twined animal entrails. The well-constructed bows of the Kutenai and other northwestern tribes were highly valued and sought after, even by Indians east of the Rockies. The arrows were a flint or wooden head fastened to a cedar shaft, with goose or chicken-hawk feathers providing the balance. The men practiced archery at every opportunity, and experts could hold five arrows in a hand and fire them with great rapidity.

A Montana Kutenai family — *Courtesy Montana Historical Society.*

The animals living within the Kutenai range were vital to the tribal economy. Both the upper and lower bands hunted deer, but the Lower Kutenai, who hunted bison far less than did their eastern fellow tribesmen, relied more heavily upon the deer for food and clothing. The Flat Bows hunted deer in communal drives directed by a deer chief who acquired his position by virtue of his hunting prowess. During a drive, young boys formed a long line and moved through wooded areas. Adult archers waited near trails to shoot the deer as they emerged. On good days, an entire season's venison could be obtained. Among the Upper Kutenai, the meat of an animal belonged solely to the man who had killed it, but the deer chief of the Lower Kutenai divided the meat equally among all the lodges.

The Kutenai also hunted elk, caribou, and moose. They especially valued the mountain goat for its fine-quality fur. They also killed muskrat and gopher for fur and food. The game birds they hunted were grouse and waterfowl. Kutenai covered their canoes with boughs for camouflage when approaching birds over water. They employed both decoys and snares in killing birds and later used the bones of waterfowl for tools, musical instruments, and moose calls.

The waters of the Kootenai River, its tributaries, and the area's lakes abounded in fish. Among the Flat Bows, fish formed a dietary staple. They trapped fish in nets and weirs built across the outlets of the sloughs and ponds left by the river's receded spring floodwater. A fishing chief supervised the building of the traps or weirs. These devices were very difficult to set and required skilled divers to secure them to the bottom of a stream. After a short period, fishermen unloaded the entrapped fish into canoes, and children emptied the canoes with special baskets. The fishing chief then directed the distribution of the fish among tribal members.

The Flat Bows periodically journeyed to the headwaters of the Columbia to fish for salmon. They usually speared the fish from their canoes at night, using torches for light. Salmon fishing was wholly an individual effort, and each man kept what he speared. The Upper Kutenai more frequently employed poles and twined bark lines for fishing, and they were especially skilled at fishing through ice.

The women cleaned and smoked or dried the fish. They preferred to dry fish in the sun on racks supported by four poles tied together like a tipi frame. They boiled the cured fish before

Kutenais of Montana's Tobacco Plains — *Courtesy Lincoln County Library, Libby, Montana.*

eating it. The Kutenai fish festival took place during each fishing season. Women prepared this feast, but only the men participated in it. Everyone carefully avoided breaking a single bone while eating his fish, because this was regarded as a bad omen for the upcoming season. Following the feast, each man examined the fish bones of those sitting next to him to make sure none was broken.

Wild roots and berries gave variety to the Kutenai diet. In early spring, when the plant was in flower, the women used pointed sticks to dig bitterroot from the dry regions around Tobacco Plains. They dried the roots and prepared them by boiling or stewing with meat. They cooked the sweeter camas root in much the same way.

The Kutenai felt that nearly every plant and root in their domain had some magical curative powers known only to the few tribal women who specialized in herbal lore. Unlike white settlers, the Indians valued the tree not for its lumber but as a source of food. From the western yellow pine they obtained cone nuts, sap, and the inner bark, which they removed with special deer-bone scrapers. The Kootenai country was rich in berries, and the Indians seasonally gathered huckleberries, choke cherries, and service berries. The black moss clinging to the branches of the region's evergreens provided them with a bread substitute. They mixed the moss with wild onions and baked it over hot rocks covered with willows and skunk cabbage leaves.

Families stored the dried roots, berries, and meat in skin bags or cedar boxes tied together with twined roots. When properly packed, stored food would last as long as two years. The main Kutenai cooking utensils were large, tightly woven baskets made of split and peeled cedar roots dyed black and green. The largest size of these held five gallons of water which was heated by throwing hot rocks into the basket. Both the Flat Bows and Horse Indians made simple wooden bowls of gouged-out log sections. They also molded and sun dried pottery from clay taken from the bed of streams. The tribe's fires, made with simple palm drills, often took more than an hour to kindle. In later years, they used flint to start fires in a matter of minutes.

The Kutenai, prior to the arrival of white missionaries, grew no food crops and raised only a small quantity of tobacco. The Tobacco Plains region on the shores of the Upper Kootenai derived its name from the kinnikinnik leaves which the Indians gathered for smoking. Even in recent times, according to one study, the Bonners Ferry Kutenai have found it difficult to adapt to farming their own lands. Although the life of the Kutenai was one of drudgery and constant struggle, famine was so unusual that they considered its origin to be supernatural.

Contributing to the Kutenais' difficult life was their total lack of metals prior to the arrival of the white man. They made wide use of the various rocks and minerals of the region in forming their tools. To make wedges or axes, they used the hardest granite and pounded it into shape on a hard bed of rock. They also made axes and knives from flint which they reinforced by rubbing with bear fat. From Pipe Creek, near present Libby, came the soft white stone from which they molded pipe bowls. Hammers consisted of a stone fastened to a stick covered with rawhide. The bones of small animals served to make needles and hooks. Food was often ground with a mortar and pestle made by pounding a hard rock onto a softer one.

The Kutenais' ability to utilize fully that which nature provided was never more evident than in their preparation of animal hides. They used the tough hides of the elk and bison for

Fort Steele, British Columbia, area Kutenais shown gathered around Chief Isodore-Kieth, 1898 — *Courtesy Provincial Archives, Victoria, British Columbia.*

lodge covers and blankets; the skin of deer and mountain sheep served as clothing. The women attached the hide to a square frame and scraped it clean of fur. They then treated it with a curing solution made by mixing wild rhubarb and horse manure in water. After drying the hide, the squaws soaked it in a solution of mashed animal brains. They smoked the hide if it was to be used for moccasins.

The Kutenai took pride in their spotless white deerskin clothing. Women's frocks and men's shirts displayed elaborate fringe work, a tribal distinguishing mark. They decorated clothing very little until later times when dyed porcupine quills and beads obtained from white traders were used. They wore several different types of headdresses, including hats of leather, fur, or horse mane. In the summer, women sometimes wore willow wreaths. Only rarely did they use feathers in any of these headdresses, although they sometimes wore headbands decorated with two or three colored feathers. Women parted their hair in the middle and wore two braids that had weasel tails tied around the ends. Both sexes wore skin mittens in winter.

The Kutenais loved color. From the Vermillion River, they obtained red clay from which they made two shades of red for painting their faces and tipis. They often used white facial paint. Their main cosmetic practice consisted of a daily bath in the nearest stream regardless of the weather. They sometimes used ointments and perfumes made from flowers. Women wore earrings and necklaces made from bears' teeth and owl feathers.

In the construction of their lodges, the Upper Kutenai showed more affinity to their eastern neighbors, the Blackfeet, than to their fellow tribesmen in the lower valley. Their standard dwelling was a tipi of elk or bison skin attached to a four-pole frame reinforced by fifteen supplementary lodge poles. Women, working in groups of four, constructed the lodges. They scraped the hides, cut them into triangular shapes, and attached them to the poles, carefully leaving a smoke hole in the uppermost skin. In winter, pegs staked the cover to the ground and prevented air from coming in through the bottom. Modern Kutenais claim that a well-made tipi was warmer than the frame houses they occupy today. Fir boughs or a deer robe carpet covered the lodge floor. The skin tipi came into wide use once the horse made the upper bands more mobile. When the Kutenais set up camp, they arranged their lodges in a circle with the chief's tipi in the center. It took an hour of hard work to erect a lodge and prepare it for occupancy.

Because of the shortage of skins and the long distances to the buffalo grounds, the Lower Kutenai used hemp matting to cover their tipis. The summer tipi was similar in design to the Upper Kutenai lodge, but in the winter, several families joined together to construct a long lodge. These houses consisted of simple bipod frames covered with the same matting used in the summer tents. A single lodge held up to eight families. In the early summer, each family took away its portion of the long house cover and built an individual tipi.

The Kutenai constructed symmetrical sweat lodges consisting of a bent willow frame covered with wet sod which prevented the steam from escaping. The lodge contained a deep hole which held hot rocks. Inside this structure, men poured water over the stones to produce steam. They remained inside as long as their bodies could tolerate the heat. The Kutenais often plunged directly from the steam bath into a cold lake or stream. They regarded such a treatment as a curative for rheumatism and other ailments.

The upper bands differed somewhat from the Flat Bows in their method of transportation. The extensive rivers of their range enabled them to cover most distances by water, but for their frequent journeys to the bison grounds, they had to rely upon overland travel methods. Even after obtaining horses, they made the winter hunt on foot, and so their snowshoes were always important. Each man made his own snowshoes from saplings bent into a circular shape enclosing a mesh of twined rawhide. Before they had horses, the Kutenai often used large dogs for pulling heavy loads.

The eastern groups were the first Kutenai to obtain horses, probably from the Shoshones early in the Eighteenth Century. They valued horses highly; a man often measured his wealth in terms of the horses he possessed. Riding equipment consisted of a simple hide bridle with reins. Usually only old people used saddles, which consisted of a wood or bone frame covered with buckskin to which looped cottonwood stirrups were attached. The travois used so extensively by the plains tribes was almost unknown to the Kutenai because of the rugged mountain terrain, although they sometimes used a crude travois to carry wounded warriors back to camp. They kept large herds of pack horses which often attracted Blackfoot raiders.

Since they seldom traveled to the bison ranges, the Flat Bows possessed far fewer horses and relied more upon water transportation than did their eastern neighbors. The Kutenai canoes, with long projections at each end, have led certain authorities to claim that they are duplicates of canoes built by the natives of Siberia's Amur Valley. The canoes consisted of a bark covering attached to a white cedar frame. For this covering, the Kutenai used a single piece of bark which he had carefully pried from the

A Lower Kutenai mat tepee — *Courtesy Lincoln County Library, Libby, Montana.*

trunk of a mountain tree. He treated it with pitch to make it waterproof. The brave paddled the canoe with a single piece of wood carved into a blade shape.

In steering his boat through the often treacherous waters of the Kootenai River, the Indian knelt directly on the canoe's bottom, with his knees spread hard against the sides for balance. The rear point served as a rudder while the front projection warded off rocks when running rapids. Kutenai bands often engaged in trade with each other, and it was not unusual to see a flotilla of more than three hundred canoes moving up or down the river.

Sometimes the Kutenai embarked on canoe trips in order to join together on festive occasions. Each season brought different ceremonies, such as the fish festival, the sun dance, the grizzly bear dance, and the midwinter festival. Tribesmen dressed in special furs, skins, and feathers to fit each occasion as they gathered on common ground for dancing and other rituals. The beat of rawhide drums accompanied the dancing and chanting, which usually lasted an entire night.

Kutenais had a sun dance chief who directed the week-long sun ceremony. This involved the erection of a fifty-foot pole and the laying of gifts before a ceremonial doll which was hidden at the end of the celebration. The grizzly bear dance took place at the beginning of each berry-picking season. Inside a special lodge, the village adults squatted in a circle, sang, danced, and smoked pipes before an altar which held the skull of a grizzly bear.

Nearly every Kutenai ceremony was a religious occasion. Even before the coming of Christianity, they believed in a master spirit who was the divine creator and guardian of mankind. The sun, moon, and stars all represented the master spirit, and through these intermediaries one could secure health, food, and shelter. They felt that all animals and objects such as rocks and water possessed spirits which could aid a person throughout his lifetime.

Upon reaching maturity, a youth journeyed to the mountains with the medicine man or shaman. Here he would be left alone for several days to await the vision of his special guardian spirit. Once this revelation had occurred, the person carried a charm of his spirit, such as a claw, feather, or twig, as a symbol of supernatural power. A man's guardian spirit was said to desert him just before death. The Kutenai believed that evil men were condemned to be ghosts on earth and that such ghosts caused much of the misery among the living. They regarded the smoking of tobacco as a means of warding off misfortune, and offered a pipe at sunrise and sunset for this purpose.

The Kutenai shaman served as a combination medicine man, prophet, spiritualist, and religious leader. He possessed certain objects known as *nupeeka* as symbols of his power. He kept secret the sources of his magic. One of his main jobs was the treatment of the sick through the use of his *nupeeka* combined with chants, dances, and the blowing of whistles. If a shaman lost many patients, it indicated that his powers were weak, and the people lost faith in his cures. In times of emergency, such as famines or game shortages, the tribe called upon the shaman to enlist the aid of the spirits. Thus, medicine men exerted a strong influence on the lives of the people, and most fathers hoped that their sons would become great shamans.

Besides the shamans, warriors who had proven themselves in battle held positions of high status in Kutenai society. The tribe engaged in war mainly to guard its range from aggression or to protect hunting parties. They rarely fought offensive wars, but individuals often "counted coup" among enemies and kept track of these hand-to-hand encounters on a notched stick. They indulged in scalping and followed up victories with the scalp dance ceremony in which braves danced and waved poles to which scalps of the slain enemy were attached.

In warfare, the Kutenai were better tacticians than most other western tribes. They posted scouts and security sentinels to prevent surprise attacks. They often surrounded the camp of the enemy for sudden raids at dawn. Once a skirmish began, all organized discipline disappeared, and each man engaged in individual coup counting. The Lower Kutenai fought very few battles, and most of these resulted from following their eastern fellow tribesmen across the mountains to hunt bison.

Kutenai camps maintained a perpetual war alert, but both men and women still managed to enjoy leisure activities. Since they usually camped on the banks of the river, they became skilled swimmers and horsemen. The men engaged in footraces, horse races, wrestling on horseback, and a hoop-ball game which resembled lacrosse. In the little leisure time that women had, they sang, danced, and played a form of cat's cradle game. The Kutenais were avid gamblers, and their games often lasted the entire night. Their most popular game involved two teams passing bone sticks as each side tried to guess which hand held the specially marked bone. A man sometimes lost all of his worldly possessions in a single game.

Young, unmarried people spent much of their leisure time in courting. The tribe revered sexual chastity, but did not pressure illegitimate parents to marry. In seeking a mate, a brave usually wanted a good worker; physical attractiveness was a secondary consideration. A man approached a girl's family directly to ask for her hand. No elaborate weddings or exchanges of gifts accompanied Kutenai unions. A couple generally lived with the wife's parents for several years before building a lodge of their own. The only marriage ceremony took place when the couple established this new residence. Politeness and mutual duties usually made mates happy together. Unlike other tribes of the region, the Kutenai did not practice polygamy, but they obtained divorces quite easily.

The family, consisting of parents and children working closely with other relatives, formed the basic Kutenai socio-economic unit. Women gathered and prepared food, tanned hides, and made the shelters, while the men hunted, fished, and guarded the camp against enemies. Beyond this, there was little division of labor. Men sometimes assisted the women in their tasks, and, in hard times, the women joined the men on hunts. Relatives usually provided for needy family members, and, if necessary, the entire band assisted in this charity.

The Kutenai had many tabus regarding pregnancy. Midwives felt that females were born after the ninth month of pregnancy, while males came after only eight months. As in most cultures, mothers loved and pampered their children. Four days after the birth of an infant, it was placed in a stiff, leather-covered cradleboard, where it remained until it began to crawl.

A boy received a bow at the age of two, and at six he was expected to kill birds to eat. Ten-year-olds could make their own bows. Girls received dolls and cradleboards at an early age. Mothers expected their daughters to prepare good meals by the age of eight. Girls usually married between sixteen and eighteen. As children grew, the father constantly gave them moral advice. In ancient times, Kutenais had only one name. With the coming of Christianity, sons and daughters often took their father's name as their last name.

Mourning accompanied death, but until the coming of the whites, funerals were not elaborate. Kutenai buried their dead flat on their backs wrapped in robes. They often painted the faces of corpses red. After the death of a family member, the survivors moved the lodge to a new location. Suicide was rare, because a person tired of life could simply go out alone against the enemy to be killed. To remarry, a widow needed the permission of the parents of her dead spouse.

Beyond the family, the Kutenai displayed a loose tribal organization. Each band had its own head chief. There was no chief to whom all tribal members owed allegiance. The head chief of the upper bands was usually the war chief. He led the tribe into battle, administered discipline, and represented the band in

Upper Kutenai tepees — *Courtesy Montana Historical Society.*

Montana Kutenais raising a Sun Dance lodge — *Courtesy Montana Historical Society.*

talks with other tribes. They held no formal elections for the head chief. He held office because of his demonstrated wisdom, bravery, and leadership in battle. The tribe rejected the idea of a hereditary chieftainship, but an old chief often appointed his son to succeed him. In cases where doubt existed as to which brave deserved the chieftainship, the shaman consulted the supernatural powers for the answer. The Upper Kutenai also had a guide chief who supervised much of the camp activity and a hunting chief who led the communal hunts. The Lower Kutenai elected their chiefs. Their band chief possessed the greatest powers of leadership, and three economic chiefs — the deer chief, fishing chief, and duck chief — directed food-gathering activities.

An informal council sometimes assisted the chief in making decisions, but the Kutenai did not form an elected tribal council until 1947. Formal social control in a camp was minimal. Since hostile enemies constantly pressed the tribe, internal unity was essential. The chief simply expelled severe wrongdoers from camp. Expulsion was tantamount to execution, and flogging was a common means of corporal punishment.

If the accounts of early white settlers and explorers in the region are accurate, the very nature of the Kutenais' character would have made camp discipline seldom necessary. Writings about the Indians abound with comments on their modesty, kindness, dignity, love of peace, and above all, their honesty. In the 1840s, Jesuit missionary Pierre Jean De Smet wrote:

Their honesty is so great and so well known, that the trader leaves his storehouse entirely, the door remaining unlocked often during his absences of weeks. The Indians go in and out and help themselves to what they need, and settle with the trader in his return . . . in doing business with them in this style he never lost the value of a pin.

Some twenty years later, British explorer John William Sullivan observed that members of the tribe never stole, seldom lied, and were strong converts to Christianity.

The Kutenais held charity in high esteem. All rich men were expected to share their possessions with those less fortunate. These people asked for very little in life and gratefully accepted the natural wealth which the Kootenai River and the surrounding country provided. They fit into nature's scheme and never sought to upset her delicate balance. By the early Nineteenth Century, however, men began arriving who viewed the Kootenai country mainly in terms of the riches which could be removed from it.

2

The Great Land Geographer

No doubt David Thompson would have rejected the title given to him by a later writer who called him "the greatest practical land geographer that the world has produced." Throughout his life, modesty and deep religious conviction characterized this London-born explorer and mapmaker. Born April 31, 1770, Thompson was the son of Welsh parents; his father died when he was seven. He attended a London school for impoverished children where he remained for seven years. He then went to work as an apprentice with the Hudson's Bay Company.

Thompson began his career in North America at Fort Churchill on the western shore of Hudson's Bay. During the following decade, he mapped the Nelson, Churchill, and Saskatchewan Rivers. After serving with Hudson's Bay Company for more than a dozen years, he felt that it offered insufficient opportunity for advancement, and so he joined forces with the Company's chief rival in British North America, the North West Company. Shortly after becoming a partner in the new organization, Thompson married Charlotte Small, a fourteen-year-old who was half Cree Indian. In 1801, she gave birth to their first child at Rocky Mountain House, the Company's post on the Saskatchewan River.

The North West Company's primary goal at the turn of the century was the establishment of trade west of the Rocky Mountains. As early as 1800, David Thompson had met a band of

Kutenai Indians at the eastern foot of the mountains. He had sent two of his men to winter with them on the western slope. These two men were probably the first whites to cross the Canadian Rockies.

The following year, Thompson made an ill-fated attempt to cross the Great Divide. Blackfeet murdered his Kutenai guide shortly after the party left Rocky Mountain House. The Cree substitute guide led them through defiles with no opening on the western slope. Thompson then spent the next five years exploring regions east of the mountains.

In 1806 the North West Company ordered him to establish trade with the tribes of the Columbia Valley. Two obstacles blocked Thompson's access to the region: the rugged terrain and hostile Piegan Blackfeet who guarded all of the main passes. It was the American explorers Lewis and Clark who removed this second barrier. In a skirmish with the Blackfeet, Meriwether Lewis killed two warriors; by late 1806, most Piegan war parties had moved south to avenge these deaths. This cleared the way for Thompson to move west.

After preparing for his journey at Rocky Mountain House, Thompson sent Jacques Raphael "Jaco" Finlay ahead with several men to blaze a trail across the mountains and to build canoes on the Columbia. Finlay, the son of a Scotch-Canadian father and a Chippewa mother, was one of the most esteemed of the North West Company's explorers and traders.

In May, 1807, Thompson embarked with his wife and three children, along with seven assistants and three pack horses. On Kootenai Plain, a wide, flat area north of the Saskatchewan River, he met and was joined by his chief assistant, Finan McDonald. McDonald had come to Canada from Scotland when his father had led a large party of highlanders to the new world. He had joined the North West Company in 1804, and following his service with Thompson, earned a reputation as an Indian fighter during an expedition into Idaho's Snake country. McDonald later served as a member of the Parliament in Upper Canada. His six-foot, four-inch height and flowing red locks contrasted sharply with Thompson's short stature and long black hair.

Thompson's party moved along a well-traveled Indian route, crossing the divide through a pass later named for the Hudson's Bay Company explorer Joseph Howse. By late June, they reached the Columbia River, which Thompson called the Kootenai. The party constructed canoes and ascended the Columbia to Windermere Lake at the river's headwaters. Here they built a post and warehouse which Thompson named "Kootenai House." The party spent a difficult winter, almost starving when a band of Blackfeet besieged the post for nearly two months. The Piegan Blackfeet had become aroused by Thompson's trading firearms

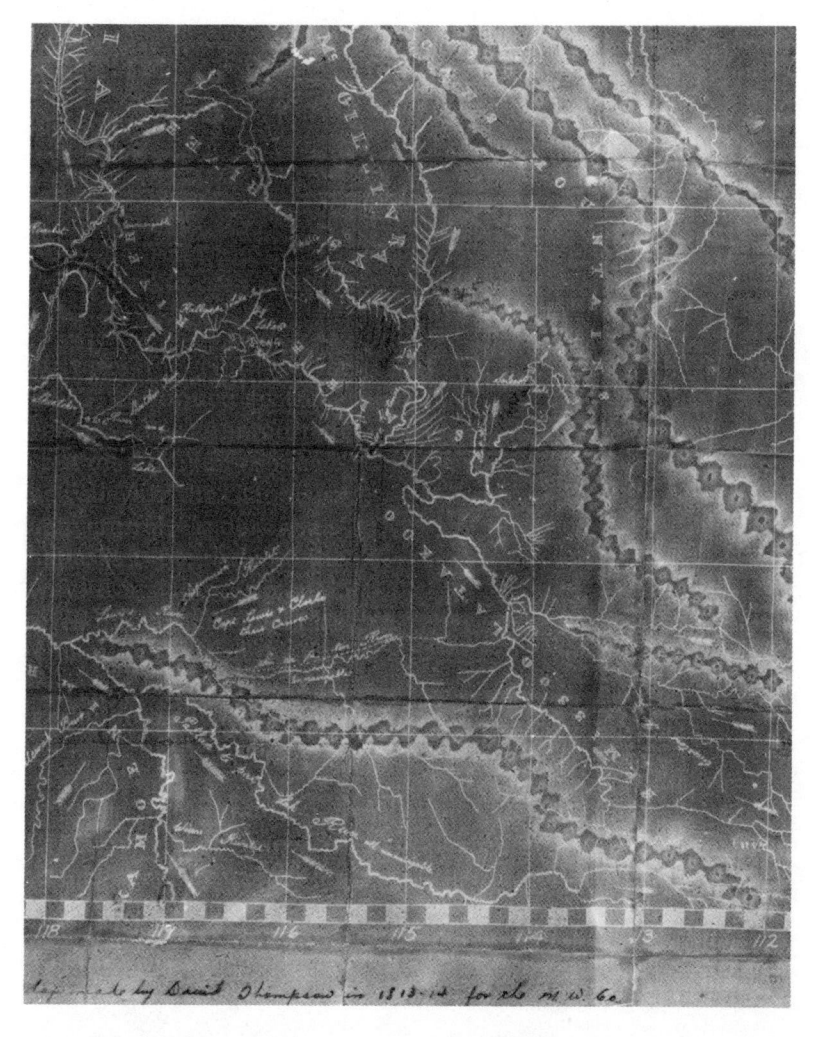

Section of David Thompson's map showing the Kootenai labeled as "McGillivray's" — *Courtesy Lincoln County Library, Libby, Montana.*

A page from David Thompson's journal — *Courtesy Lincoln County Library, Libby, Montana.*

with their enemies, the Kutenais. It took stern warnings and generous gifts to thwart a major attack on Kootenae House later that winter.

In April, 1808, Thompson left McDonald in charge of Kootenae House. With four men, he canoed south to a level area at the head of Columbia Lake, which he named "McGillivray's Portage" after the head of the North West Company, William McGillivray. It was here that Thompson became the first white man to discover both the source of the Columbia and the main channel of the Kootenai. The party crossed the narrow portage and moved down the Kootenai River which Thompson also named after McGillivray. During this trip he recorded in his journal:

I observed the River in general has a very smooth easy current with a sufficient depth of water, and where we are camped the points are of fine meadow and the first ground I have seen that has sufficient moisture to farm.

On this trip, as on many of their journeys, Thompson and his men lived frequently on the verge of starvation. They killed and ate a mountain lion which Thompson called "very good food," even though the men who ate it experienced violent headaches for several hours. On May 6, after the portage around Kootenai Falls, the party encountered a camp of Flat Bow Indians near present Bonners Ferry, Idaho. The Indians could give the hungry travelers only some moss bread and dried carp, and so they moved downstream to Kootenay Lake. Near the Lake, Thompson found river navigation very dangerous because of violent eddies and whirlpools, and it took hard paddling to escape destruction. In the area of modern Creston, Thompson observed that the flooded river flowed across extensive meadows. They found it futile to attempt to proceed down the overflowing waters, and so with the assistance of Indian guides, they returned on horseback to Kootenae House.

Flooding streams and a shortage of food hampered their northward trek. At one point sharp rocks cut the horses feet so severely that Thompson later recalled, "they could be traced by their blood." After moving up the Moyie River, they reached the Kootenai near Wild Horse Creek, where Thompson built a canoe. The weary party then paddled upstream, recrossed McGillivray's Portage, and reached Kootenae House in early June. During this first known journey by a white man down the valley of the Kootenai, Thompson took careful geographical notes and recorded all of the plant and animal species he encountered. His journals also gave the earliest written account of navigation on the Kootenai.

After taking a load of furs back across the Rockies, Thompson returned to Kootenae House late in October. He then sent Finan McDonald and a party back down the Kootenai to establish trade relations with the Indians. Unseasonable cold and ice in the river plagued McDonald's group. On the river's north bank above Kootenai Falls opposite present Libby, Montana, McDonald and his crew constructed a log storehouse. They spent the winter in two leather tents. This post was the first commercial establishment in western Montana. Later, another North West Company explorer, James McMillan, joined McDonald, and they conducted the region's first trade transactions. Not until several years later did the North West Company establish a permanent post on the Kootenai near present Jennings, Montana.

A devout Anglican, David Thompson forbade the use of alcohol in any of his trading. Prior to one of his trips across the Rocky Mountains, his partners obliged him to haul two kegs of liquor west. Thompson had the kegs tied to a horse which he knew to be wild. The animal immediately banged the kegs on nearby rocks and got rid of his load. Not another gallon of alcohol went west during Thompson's tenure.

In July 1809, after returning from another trek to Rocky Mountain House, Thompson again moved down the Kootenai. During this trip, he became the first white man to attempt farming along the river, as he sowed a small number of seeds on Tobacco Plains. This garden had virtually no chance for survival, as Thompson discovered on his return trip.

The party then moved down the Kootenai as far as the Bonners Ferry region. From there, they proceeded south on an Indian trail, the "Great Road of the Flatheads." On Lake Pend Orielle, Thompson began dealing with the Flathead Indians and constructed the trading post he called Kullyspel House. He then rode more than fifty miles up the Clark Fork of the Columbia and crossed back north to the Kootenai where he met James McMillan bringing down more trade goods. The two men descended the Kootenai and returned to Kullyspel House. In November 1809, Thompson again traveled up the Clark Fork to the area near present Thompson Falls, Montana. Here he built another trading post, the Saleesh House, where he spent the winter.

Hudson's Bay Company pathfinder, Joseph Howse — *Courtesy Provincial Archives, Victoria, British Columbia.*

By 1810, the rival Hudson's Bay Company became so curious about Thompson's trading ventures that they sent their man, Joseph Howse, to check up on activities west of the mountains. Howse, with nine other men, crossed the pass which would later bear his name and followed Thompson's route down the Kootenai and across to the Clark Fork. They established a small trading post just north of Flathead Lake. By early 1811, Hudson's Bay Company decided to end competition in the Columbia region, and so Howse abandoned the post, never to return.

Thompson, meanwhile, made another trip east in 1810 only to be sent back west by the North West Company; his superiors wanted him to reach the mouth of the Columbia before the

A memorial to David Thompson at the site of Kootenae House, British Columbia — *Courtesy Provincial Archives, Victoria, British Columbia.*

American Astorian traders could claim the area. Thompson found hostile Blackfeet blocking his return through Howse Pass. After wasting three weeks deciding what to do, Thompson abandoned his planned route. The party went north where they crossed the mountains at Athabaska Pass. Deep snow slowed their advance and forced them to leave their horses and to build sleds and make snowshoes. Desertions decimated the original twenty-four man group. At the junction of the Wood and Columbia Rivers, they erected a cabin and spent the winter. This detour cost Thompson and his men valuable time in their efforts to reach the Columbia's mouth before representatives from the American Astorian Company.

During the following April, the crew built a large cedar canoe and moved up the Columbia to its headwaters. They carried the canoe across the flats and proceeded down the Kootenai as far as the loop of the river. Here they crossed overland to Saleesh House. Thompson was as anxious to survey the lower Columbia as he was to secure the trade outlet for the North West Company. He built another cedar canoe and floated down the Clark Fork and Columbia, mapping the region. In July of 1811, his party reached the Columbia's mouth, where the rival Americans of the Pacific Fur Company greeted them at the newly built Fort Astoria. After a sojourn of two weeks, they moved back up the Columbia and eventually ended a difficult voyage at the mouth of the Canoe River. This completed Thompsons' navigation and survey of the Columbia River's entire length.

After a brief trip across the Rockies and back, Thompson descended the Columbia with trade goods. He spent the autumn and winter transporting supplies to Spokane House north of the lower Columbia and trading from Saleesh House on the Clark Fork. In May of 1812, David Thompson left the Columbia-Kootenai country via Athabaska Pass, never to return.

Back in Montreal, Thompson constructed his amazingly accurate map of North America. For seventy-five years, it served as a standard reference for western Canada, and it remains a monument to his remarkable surveying skill and his indomitable will. Unfortunate business transactions and debts incurred by his sons forced him to live his last years in poverty. He died in 1857 and was buried in an unmarked grave. Not even a paragraph in the local press noted his passing, yet his work was unparalleled in the history of exploration and geography. He had surveyed and mapped the vast region from Hudson's Bay to the Pacific Ocean, discovered the Kootenai River and the source of the Columbia, and charted the entire course of each river. He laid the foundation for North West Company's fur monopoly in the Columbia and Kootenai area for an entire decade. All of this remained virtually unknown, until the rediscovery of his achievements early in the twentieth century. Only then did men rightfully claim David Thompson as one of the world's foremost geographers and explorers.

3

Mountaineers and Missionaries

Following David Thompson's departure, the North West Company, under John George McTavish, continued to trade west of the Rockies. The Kootenai River served as an important transportation artery for the fur trade, but the Company concentrated its main efforts to the south in the valleys of the Clark Fork and Snake Rivers where furs were more plentiful. Traders abandoned Howse Pass in favor of the Athabaska route through the mountains, taking them farther away from the Kootenai. Thompson's Kootenae House therefore fell into disuse. Nicholas Montour supervised the Company's remaining trade in the Columbia and Kootenai regions.

In 1812, the North West Company began to feel competition from the Astorian traders based at the mouth of the Columbia. The Americans sent Donald McKenzie into the Snake River region to establish trading posts among the Flatheads and Couer d'Alenes. They also sent Francis Benjamin Pillet into the Kootenai Valley where he and Montour engaged in a bitter rivalry which ended on the dueling field. Their encounter had a less than tragic outcome when one man was shot through the coat collar and the other received a bullet in the trouser leg. A tailor mended their "wounds," and the two departed friends.

After the outbreak of the War of 1812, McTavish informed the Astorians that the North West traders would oppose them with arms if necessary. This, coupled with a lack of provisions and a disappointing interior trade, led the Americans to sell out their property to the British and to abandon the Columbia region. This left the North West Company with a monopoly of the fur trade in the area, which it retained until its 1821 merger with the Hudson's Bay Company.

Following the merger, the Columbia and Kootenai continued to serve as transportation routes for furs and company personnel. Trading boats on these rivers were frail craft manned by a bowman, steersman, and middle men. Before descending rapids, the steersman landed the craft to inspect the river, making sure that it was safe to proceed. The bowman stood at the prow of the craft and used a long pole to steer clear of rocks. A tow line pulled the boat upstream through rapids.

Fur traders found life in the wilds lonely and full of danger. Their need for companionship led many to take their Indian wives along on their trips into the mountains. These women performed some of the most difficult tasks during the expeditions. Nearly all traders felt duty-bound to educate their half-Indian children, even on the difficult trips.

During the 1820s, the Kootenai River remained relatively free of whites except for the passage of an occasional trapper or explorer such as the Scottish botanist, David Douglas. The man for whom the Douglas fir was named moved up the Columbia in 1827, studying the flora and fauna of the Pacific Northwest. He camped near the mouth of the Kootenai which he described as "a stream of considerable magnitude, rapid and very clear." He then proceeded up the Columbia and across Athabasca Pass.

During the 1820s and 1830s, American fur men based at St. Louis threatened the Hudson's Bay dominance of the Northwest trade. The Americans, however, felt that the Kootenai held little value, and so they remained out of the area. During this period, many Kutenai Indian traders journeyed to the Flathead country to rendezvous with Hudson's Bay brigades. They traded their furs very cheaply, as they wanted only ammunition and tobacco.

In 1828, William Kittson of the Hudson's Bay Company built a fur collection depot which became known as Fort Kootenai near the present town of Libby, Montana. In 1846, Edward Berland moved Fort Kootenai north to Tobacco Plains. During the next fifteen years, traders moved this post several times, but it remained in the same general region. After Berland's death, John Linklater took charge of the post and spent twelve winters there. In 1858, a contemporary noted that all trade at Fort Kootenai was

Explorer and botanist, David Douglas — *Courtesy Provincial Archives, Victoria, British Columbia.*

conducted in beaver skins. One fur brought thirty charges of powder and thirty bullets, and ten pelts paid for a musket. Three bear skins could be traded for a blanket.

In the years following 1835, the British fur trade throughout the area steadily declined, until by 1845 the take totaled about one-tenth the amount of twenty years earlier. The head of the Hudson's Bay Company during this period was Sir George Simpson, a renowned explorer and traveler. In 1841 during a trip around the world, Simpson and his party crossed the Kootenai country. They reached the Kootenai Valley from the Vermillion River, crossed Vermillion Pass, and moved up the Columbia to Columbia Lake. Here they discovered the hot springs long visited by the Indians and today known as Fairmont. They followed the Kootenai River south to the Cranbrook region from where they moved across to the Moyie River. It took the party more than six weeks to cross the Kootenai area, which Simpson later described as "extremely rugged and precipitous" and filled with "thick forests, deep morasses," and "stupendous rocks." He concluded that any large-scale attempt by Englishmen to exploit or settle this underdeveloped region would only attract the attention of the Americans.

In 1846, the Anglo-American Oregon Treaty divided both the upper and lower Kootenai at the forty-ninth parallel. Still, for many years the line remained unsurveyed, and Indians, traders, and missionaries crossed it freely.

From their earliest contacts with the trappers, the Kutenais had learned of the new religion of the whites. Most likely they first heard about Christianity from the Iroquois employees of the Hudson's Bay Company. For years, the Kutenais expressed a desire to learn more about the Christian faith, but for years, their requests for missionaries went unheeded.

Not until 1838 was the first Christian church service held in their domain when the Quebec priests Blanchet and Demers celebrated a mass on the upper Columbia and baptized several Indian children. Other than this and a few brief Jesuit missionary visits, Kutenai calls for religious instruction were in vain.

Father Pierre Jean De Smet did more than any other white man to convert the Kutenais to Christianity. In 1840, this Belgium-born Jesuit began living among the Salish at St. Mary's Mission which he established in the Bitterroot Valley of Montana. He first contacted the Kutenais in the winter of 1841—1842 when he baptized many of their number near Flathead Lake.

In 1845, armed only with a rosary and a crucifix, De Smet and his two Indian guides embarked from St. Ignatius Mission in the Flathead country and moved north. His goal was to meet and convert both the Kutenai and Blackfeet Indians. Like David Thompson, De Smet was an avid geographer, and he recorded much of what he saw in the Columbia and Kootenai Valleys.

The priest reached the Kootenai near the Idaho-Montana border, where he wrote:

The river is, in this place, deep and tranquil, moving along with a steady pace until aroused from its inertness by the universal thaws; it then descends with such astounding impetuosity that it destroys the banks and in its furious course, uproots and bears along trees, fragments of rocks, and c., which vainly oppose its passage.

Jesuit missionary Jean Pierre de Smet — *Courtesy Provincial Archives, Victoria, British Columbia.*

The first band of Indians De Smet encountered eagerly embraced the faith, and he shared in their annual fish festival before advancing up the river. Of the Montana section of the Kootenai he observed, "the entire tract . . . seems awaiting the benign influence of a civilized people." At Tobacco Plains, he visited another Kutenai band which received him with "joy and filial affection." Here he baptized many tribesmen and erected a large cross. Although short of food, the Indians pressed him to remain several days among them. He secured the services of two Kutenai guides to escort him to the land of the Blackfeet.

Proceeding north through the densely timbered valley, De Smet reached McGillivray's Portage and crossed over to the headwaters of the Columbia. Here he encountered the Canadian trader, Francois Morigeau, whom the Jesuit described as "the monarch who rules over the source of the Columbia." After spending several days with Morigeau, the missionary moved east to the upper reaches of the Kootenai where he observed, "innumerable torrents rushed headlong with a thousand mazes from the mountain's brow."

De Smet spent much of the winter east of the Rockies and returned to the Columbia basin the following spring. On his journey down the Columbia, he visited the Flat Bows near the mouth of the Kootenai. Throughout his travels, the Jesuit had found many of the Indians already praying together. When he revisited a group of Kutenais over a decade later, they still adhered to the rituals he had taught them.

During the 1850s, Father Joseph Menetrey of St. Ignatius Mission periodically visited the Tobacco Plains Kutenais. In 1857, the tribe built a log chapel which Menetrey and other missionaries frequented. In 1873, north of the border, the Order of Oblates of eastern Canada led by Father Leon Fouquet founded St. Eugene's Mission at the junction of the St. Mary's and Kootenai Rivers. The Indians set up their lodges in the area, and Father Fouquet brought in cattle and supervised farming activities.

Besides the missionaries, several parties of explorers and settlers crossed the Kootenai country in the 1840s and 1850s. In the mid-1850s, Isaac Stevens and James Doty on separate expeditions traversed the southern Kootenai Valley while searching for low mountain passes for possible railroad routes. In 1854, the renowned army surveyor Lieutenant John Mullan approached the region from the south but did not explore the valley extensively.

On the Canadian side, Hudson's Bay Company's Sir George Simpson, alarmed by the number of American immigrants pouring into the Oregon country, moved to induce British settlers to travel westward. Lured by Simpson's offers of livestock, seed, and housing in exchange for a portion of their crops, twenty-three families led by Hudson's Bay clerk James Sinclair moved west from Manitoba in 1841. They carried their belongings on canvas-covered, two-wheeled carts which they abandoned upon reaching the mountains. They crossed the Great Divide near the headwaters of the Kootenai and followed the river upstream before turning westward to the Columbia Valley. They proceeded south to Walla Walla, Washington, via the same Moyie River route Simpson had pioneered on his around-the-world trip. The company proved unable to live up to its promises, and most of the settlers became American citizens.

Reverend Leon Fouquet of St. Eugenes Mission — *Courtesy Provincial Archives, Victoria, British Columbia.*

In 1854, Sinclair led a second expedition which included members of his own family. They crossed the Kootenai near McGillivray's Portage and went down the river along the same route pioneered by David Thompson in 1808. They traded livestock for Kutenai Indian horses, giving the tribe the first cattle it ever possessed. At Fort Kootenai on Tobacco Plains, John Linklater greeted them. The settlers continued to follow the river until they cut south toward the Spokane region.

Three years after Sinclair's second expedition, the British government appointed an Imperial Commission to investigate the suitability of western Canada for settlement and the feasibility of a transcontinental railway. Captain John Palliser took charge of the exploration of the area, with the assistance of geologist James Hector, astronomer John William Sullivan, meteorologist

Father Nicholas Coccola of St. Eugenes Mission — *Courtesy Provincial Archives, Victoria, British Columbia.*

St. Eugenes Mission Church — *Courtesy Provincial Archives, Victoria, British Columbia.*

Hudson's Bay Company official and reknowned traveler Sir George Simpson — *Courtesy Provincial Archives, Victoria, British Columbia.*

Thomas Blakiston, and French botanist Eugene Bourgeau. Palliser, a British nobleman, had originally planned to undertake the expedition at his own expense. Upon learning of his plans, the Royal Geographical Society persuaded the British Colonial Office to grant him five thousand pounds to cover expenses.

Traveling mostly over the well-trodden trails of the Indians and fur traders, the Palliser expedition reached the Rocky Mountains in June 1858. Constant quarreling, especially between Sullivan and the headstrong Blakiston, plagued the project from the start. Angered because Palliser had named Hector as his second in command, Blakiston soon separated from the main party and became the first known white man to cross Kootenai Pass. He then moved southeast across the international boundary into the upper Flathead Valley. After camping at Fort Kootenai, his party returned north down the Kootenai River and east across Kootenai Pass. Meanwhile, Palliser's party explored the Continental Divide country farther north. After a fruitless search for

Canadian Kootenai pathfinders Captain John Palliser and Dr. James Hector — *Courtesy Provincial Archives, Victoria, British Columbia.*

more passes across the Rockies, his group also returned by way of Kootenai Pass.

The following spring, the Palliser party, now minus both Bourgeau and Blakiston, again set out to explore the Kootenai Country. The group numbered eighteen men, including several American prospectors and two Indians. Palliser followed the Kootenai River from the base of the Rockies clear to Kootenay Lake where he feasted on salmon with Indian hosts. He then moved down the lower Kootenai and Columbia Rivers to Fort Colville. From there he sent Sullivan back to the Kootenai to explore the country around the Moyie Lakes. Sullivan's route up the Salmon River later became a railway and highway route.

During that same summer, the party's geologist, Dr. Hector, explored the country between the upper Columbia and upper Kootenai. He found very few good trails there because the Indians no longer inhabited the area. He proceeded south to Fort Kootenai where Linklater supplied him with provisions for his passage to Fort Colville. Here he rejoined Palliser, and the entire party then sailed for England from America's west coast.

The Palliser expedition clearly mapped the major passes of the Canadian Rockies. Bourgeau collected more than ten thousand specimens of plant life, and the explorers carefully recorded geological and meteorological observations. Of equal significance, the party's relations with the Indians were cordial, and there were no incidents of violence.

James Sinclair, leader of settlers through the Kootenai country —
Courtesy Provincial Archives, Victoria, British Columbia.

Not all such white encounters with Indians on the Kootenai were so peaceful. In 1848, British traders William Hamilton and Alex McKay joined a large Kutenai hunting party which had been chased by Blackfeet from the Glacier Park area across the mountains to Tobacco Plains. Here they met their pursuers near Fort Kootenai. During the ensuing skirmish, the Kutenais drove the Blackfeet into a timbered area from where they managed to escape back across the mountains. In this incident, one of the few recorded armed clashes on the Kootenai involving whites and Indians, the whites sided with the Kutenais against the tribe's ancient enemies.

Relations between the Kutenais and whites, however, were not entirely cordial during this period. In July 1855, the Kutenais, along with the Flatheads and Upper Pend D'Orielles, negotiated with Governor Isaac Stevens of Washington Territory, which then included Idaho and Montana. Governor Stevens sought to persuade all three tribes to move onto a designated reservation, but the chiefs could not agree on a single location. Once the Flathead Reservation had been established, the government, in effect, told the Kutenais either to move onto it or go north to Canada.

Chief Michelle, who had represented the Kutenais at the parley, had vainly hoped for a single great Kutenai reserve where all bands could live together and practice their old life style. After the treaty, some of the tribesmen moved to the reservation at Elmo and Dayton, Montana. Disillusioned, Michelle and his followers traveled up the Kutenai to Windermere, British Columbia, where they formed a new band. The Bonners Ferry group of Lower Kutenai under Chief Abraham claimed that Michelle had not represented them at the Stevens meeting. They remained on their old domain as non-treaty Indians until 1895 when the United States Government gave them a small land allotment. The condition of the Kutenais on the Flathead reservation soon degenerated as government agents adopted an expedient policy of temporary, stop gap relief. By 1873, reservation Kutenais owned sixty acres of land, while the other two reservation tribes possessed more than one thousand acres.

Not until the 1880s did the Canadian Government establish several reserves for the tribe in both east and west Kootenai. Chief David of Canada's upper Kootenai expressed the feelings of many fellow tribesmen on both sides of the border. During negotiations with the British Columbia Indian Superintendent, he pointed out:

If I came to your country and asked you to pick out land for a reserve you would not like it. You would refuse because you would know you were to pick out land of what was already yours.

4

Wild Horse

By the early 1860s, the Kootenai Valley lay silent and undisturbed — virtually the same state in which it had been prior to the invasion of the fur traders. Only old Fort Kootenai on the Tobacco Plains plus a few half-white sons of fur trappers gave testimony to the fact that whites had ever been there.

Palliser's geologist, James Hector, writing in 1859, noted that a small amount of gold had been taken from the bed of the Kootenai near Tobacco Plains, but such experiments were undertaken out of "curiosity." It was in 1863 that Jaco Finlay, the half-Indian son of David Thompson's aide, wandering along one of the small tributaries of the upper Kootenai, discovered placer gold in the sandy stream bottom. He took his gold dust and nuggets to Fort Kootenai, where John Linklater transported them to Fort Colville. Here news of the find spread and touched off a rush of hundreds of Americans into the heretofore peaceful valley.

The lucky few who were first to reach the region of the find included Dave Griffith, James Manning, and Robert Dore. The richest placer lay along a small tributary of the Kootenai fifty miles north of the international boundary. This stream was known as Wild Horse Creek because of the abundance of horses in the region.

By late summer of 1864, hundreds had staked their claims, and more than a thousand miners had settled along some four miles of the creek. Most came north from Idaho and Montana where diggings had begun to play out. The influx of miners led the

Hudson's Bay Company to move its trading post from Fort Kootenai to the Wild Horse region and to place Michael Phillips in charge. Phillips became one of the first homesteaders to take up land on the Kootenai, and later discovered the famous Crows Nest Pass, along with its abundant coal fields. A roaring camp sprang up on the creek. In the autumn of 1864, Colonial Secretary Arthur N. Birch, who had traveled to Wild Horse from Victoria, reported that the new town had three restaurants, a large brewery, and numerous saloons serving the miners.

Men kept records of their debts with merchants during the week, and on Sunday everyone paid their bills. The prospectors usually destroyed these records, so the amount of gold taken from the region has never been determined accurately. Estimates run as high as fifteen million dollars. One nugget alone weighed more than thirty-six ounces and was valued at nearly seven hundred dollars.

Most miners who moved up the Kootenai were young men, bearded, and dressed in flannel shirts, pants, hob-nailed boots, and broad-brimmed felt hats. They survived on a steady diet of salt pork, beans, and coffee, and diseases such as scurvy and rheumatism were common. They were a restless breed, and the slightest rumor of a new strike sent them moving to another creek. Since lumber was scarce, most of them built their crude cabins from logs. They used baked clay for the chimneys. Floors of dirt were common.

Basic mining tools included a pick, shovel, and gold pan. Prospectors either panned in the streams or dug through the shallow soil to the blue slate bedrock. A few dug long ditches or sank shafts, but this required a capital outlay that most gold seekers lacked. Robert Dore installed one of the first hydraulic mining operations in British Columbia, using a large hose freighted from San Francisco.

When the first miners clamored up the Kootenai from the United States, the nearest law officer and jail were almost a month's ride away. To uphold the law, many prospectors banded together and drew up a legal code which they planned to enforce on their own. Soon, however, Judge Peter O'Reilly reached the region from the west coast; he assembled the miners at the small log cabin which served as a courthouse. Standing near a flagpole which flew the Union Jack, he proclaimed:

Boys, I am here to keep order and administer the law. Those who

Wild Horse Judge Peter O'Reilly — *Courtesy Provincial Archives, Victoria, British Columbia.*

don't want law and order can "git," but those who stay with the camp remember on what side of the line the camp is for. Boys, if there is shooting in the Kootenay there will be hanging in the Kootenay.

Throughout the boom only two recorded fatal shootings occurred in Wild Horse. The first came during a July Fourth celebration in 1864, when Thomas Walker shot the thumb off Yeast Powder Bill after a drunken quarrel. Bill retaliated by fatally shooting Walker. The twelve-man jury acquitted Bill, but they gave him thirty minutes to leave the camp, which he promptly did.

The other murder involved the shooting of Constable Jack Lawson by a horse thief named Brown. An Indian reported the

47

Kootenai government official and founder of Fernie, British Columbia, William Fernie — *Courtesy Provincial Archives, Victoria, British Columbia.*

incident, and a miners' posse finally caught up with Brown and hanged him in Idaho.

More common than murder was the type of crime practiced by "Little Lou," a dancehall girl who was said to have been equally adroit at stealing pokes of gold dust, singing sentimental ballads, and delivering testimonials at camp meetings. Most of the cases in O'Reilly's court involved claim jumping and boundary disputes.

For thieves and miners alike, the Wild Horse excitement proved short-lived. In 1865, after a hungry winter, the shallow diggings rapidly disappeared. The restless Americans put on snowshoes and moved north to another rumored strike at the Big Bend of the Columbia. They left Wild Horse Creek to be worked over by the more patient Chinese. The Orientals bought up the old claims and by hard work thrived in the area for many years. By 1866, the population of Wild Horse totaled one hundred whites and about three hundred Chinese. The Kootenai's first mining rush had ended.

From Wild Horse, many prospectors drifted to nearby streams. In 1867, Frank Perry, Dan Kennedy, and others found rich ore on a creek which soon bore Perry's name. Miners claimed fifteen miles of the creek, but this soon also proved to be of short duration.

On the loop of the Kootenai, a group led by veteran prospector Jack Fisher was panning for gold when they learned of the Wild Horse find; they rushed north. After considerable success in Canada, many returned to the southern Kootenai. One member

Placer mines on Wild Horse Creek — *Courtesy Provincial Archives, Victoria, British Columbia.*

of the party, Steven Allen, named Libby Creek after his daughter. In the summer of 1866, Allen and several other prospectors camped near this stream. A small band of three Bonners Ferry Kutenai, hunting in the same section, came upon the miners and decided to frighten them away in order to steal their provisions. They fired a volley of shots over the camp, but the miners refused to flee. The Indians then fired directly at the prospectors, killing all but one man, Joe Herring, who managed to escape despite serious wounds. A vigilante committee of miners assisted by Kutenai Chief Abraham soon rounded up the three culprits. They hanged two and shot the other when he tried to escape.

A restored miner's cabin in Libby, Montana — *Courtesy Lincoln County Library, Libby, Montana.*

For ten years after this incident, few whites entered the Montana Kootenai country. Harsh winters, hordes of mosquitoes, and isolation all helped dissuade people from settling in the area.

Isolation made supplying the Kootenai miners a major undertaking. Nearly all of the supplies to the Wild Horse mines came by pack train from the United States. Most goods flowed from Walla Walla and Spokane, but several pack trains moved up the Flathead Valley from Missoula and Kalispell, Montana. A few enterprising merchants drove beef cattle all the way from Salt Lake City through the Tobacco Plains. The provisions from Washington came via Lake Pend d'Orielle, Bonners Ferry, and up the Moyie Valley. This trip usually took twenty-five days and could be made only in summer.

As might be expected, freight rates were high, and this made supplies costly for the miners. A Wild Horse prospector could expect to spend a dollar and a half for a pound of butter, one dollar a pound for bacon, and two and a half dollars for a plug of tobacco.

The trail from Walla Walla crossed the Kootenai River in two places. At the loop in Idaho, New York native Edwin L. Bonner observed the Indians canoeing some of the first Wild Horse miners across the river. He decided that a ferry here would make far more money with less risk than prospecting. In 1864, he obtained a ferry license from Idaho Territory and hired John Walton to operate it. Nine years later, Bonner sold his business to Richard Fry, a pioneer of the area who had run supply trains from Washington to Wild Horse. Fry established a trading post at the site where he and his Indian wife and family remained for many years, packing, trading for furs, and exploring along the Kootenai.

The trail crossed the river in a second place near the mouth of Wild Horse Creek. Here John and Robert Galbraith, the sons of a Dublin professor, opened a ferry, store, and pack-train business. They charged miners one dollar for horses and five dollars for

Hon. Edgar Dewdney — *Courtesy Provincial Archives, Victoria, British Columbia.*

Thomas Hammill, killed by R. E. Sproule in a mining dispute —
Courtesy Provincial Archives, Victoria, British Columbia.

men to cross the stream. In the early 1870s, Hudson's Bay Company sold its interest on the eastern Kootenai to the Galbraiths, and for many years they held virtually a monopoly on trade in the sparsely settled section.

British Columbia officials recognized that during the Wild Horse gold rush the Kootenai area had become "Americanized." They pressed to establish a trade and communications link between the coastal cities of the province and the western mines. In 1865, the provincial governor ordered Edgar Dewdney to construct a trail from Princeton, British Columbia, to Wild Horse — a distance of 291 miles, all within Canada. Dewdney hired two hundred Chinese at seventy-five dollars a month to build the four-foot-wide trail. The construction crew followed the route blazed earlier by John Sullivan. At Fort Shepherd, near Kootenay Lake, many abandoned their work to pan for gold, but Dewdney still finished his project by September.

Miners were already leaving Wild Horse by the time of the Dewdney Trail's completion. The route crossed many rivers but had no bridges. Shortly after it opened, the Goat River swept two packers downstream, drowning one of their horses. Winter

Construction on the Dewdney Trail — *Courtesy Provincial Archives, Victoria, British Columbia.*

snows and spring floods made it impassable, and by the late 1860s, it fell into total disuse.

The abandonment of the Dewdney Trail was indicative of the virtual evacuation of the entire Kootenai Valley throughout the 1870s. In the loop section, Dick Fry continued to run his ferry and store, but he had few visitors. To the east, many of the Indians had left for the Flathead Reservation, and the area continued to be called the "Montana Wilds" well into the 1880s.

On Kootenay Lake, the Hudson's Bay Company abandoned its district headquarters post in 1870. Two years later, it burned to the ground. On the eastern branch, Wild Horse remained the governmental seat for East and West Kootenay and continued to send representatives to the Provincial Legislature. In 1874, the

Blue Bell mine on Kootenay Lake shore — *Courtesy Provincial Archives, Victoria, British Columbia.*

section had only thirty-five voters; eight years later, that number had dwindled to eleven. Several mining claims continued to be worked, but the 1879 report of government agent William Fernie explained the situation well:

I am sorry to be unable to report any improvement in the prospects of the mines in this section of British Columbia. There has been very little prospecting done this year and nothing found.

The towering mountains which sloped to the shores of the Kootenai still contained huge untapped reservoirs of mineral wealth. Their development only awaited men with sufficient capital, enterprise, and imagination to make them pay off. Such men were not long in coming.

5

The Second Mining Boom

Among the reasons for the brevity of the Wild Horse gold rush was the quality of the pay dirt gravel in the region. It was concrete-hard, and only heavy machinery and big money — things the first placer miners lacked — could make such ground yield its riches.

At the foundation of the second Kootenai mining boom was large-scale capital which came mostly from Spokane interests backed by New York dollars. As in the days of Wild Horse, American men, resources, and energy dominated the Canadian Kootenai in the 1880s. Not until the last years of the Nineteenth Century did Canadian capital and economic institutions begin to displace the Americans.

Americans with strong cultural ties to their native country filled the mine and mill towns along the river and lake. These settlers peacefully conformed to British law in most cases. The Canadian boom towns experienced far fewer violent outbreaks than did the camps south of the boundary, partially because provincial officials handled the administration of local government.

But violence marred the first important ore discovery in the Kootenay Lake area. For years, the Indians and fur trappers had visited a large outcropping of silver-lead ore, the "Big Ledge," on the eastern shore of the lake. There they had gathered lead to mold their bullets. Then, until the 1870s, the ore lay untouched.

55

Silver King mine near Nelson, British Columbia — *Courtesy Provincial Archives, Victoria, British Columbia.*

Silver King mine — *Courtesy Provincial Archives, Victoria, British Columbia.*

Early in that decade, American mine speculator George Hearst tried and failed to develop the deposit. His main problem was the inaccessibility of Kootenay Lake. The rapids between the lake and the river's junction with the Columbia proved impossible to navigate.

In 1882, an American, Robert E. Sproule, and two companions rediscovered the Big Ledge. Under Canadian law, Sproule had to register his claim and not be absent from it for more than seventy-two hours. This proved impossible because the nearest gold commissioner lived more than 240 miles away in Wild Horse. Undaunted, Sproule began working his unregistered claim.

About this time, a Portland financier, Captain George Ainsworth, also showed an interest in Kootenay Lake. He employed a young prospector, Thomas Hammil, to search for ore along the shores of the Lake. Hammil arrived at Sproule's diggings accompanied by the gold commissioner and promptly registered a legal claim. To settle their rival claims, the two parties summoned Judge Edward Kelly into the region. To show his impartiality, Kelly ate at the camp of one group and slept in the camp of the other. After a long court session, he decided in favor of Sproule's claim. Hammil appealed the decision to a higher court which reversed Kelly's judgment and forced Sproule to pay the court costs.

The disgruntled Sproule then decided to settle the matter on his own. On June 1, 1885, he hid in the bushes near the place where Hammil was mining and shot his rival, killing him instantly. After being chased for a long distance south along the Kootenai, Sproule accidently wandered into the camp of the constable and his posse of Indians. They took their prisoner to Victoria where he was tried and hanged.

The Kootenai Mining and Smelting Company, under W.A. Hendryx of Sandpoint, Idaho, then took over the ore body which had become known as the Blue Bell Mine. Development was slow until the 1895 construction of a smelter at Pilot Bay on the shore of the lake. Scows transported ore eight miles from the mine to the mill. At one time, the smelter employed two hundred men, but it was never a financial success. It fell into disuse several years after it opened. The mine was operated sporadically well into the Twentieth Century; the Consolidated Mining and Smelting Company took it over in 1931.

Equal in impact to the Blue Bell was the 1886 discovery by the

Hall brothers of Colville, Washington. They had gone north with their families, panning for gold in the streams along the way. After traveling down the Salmon River, they ended up behind Toad Mountain near the west arm of Kootenay Lake. Here three young boys in the party, while rounding up stray horses, stopped to throw stones at a covey of grouse. They noticed that the rocks were rich in copper ore. The Halls packed as much of the ore as possible back to Colville and returned the following spring to work the claim. Other miners rushed into the area, and the town which eventually became Nelson soon arose.

Pioneer builder of Nelson, British Columbia, Gilbert Malcolm Sproat—
Courtesy Provincial Archives, Victoria, British Columbia.

Laid out in 1887 by Gilbert M. Sproat, the "Queen City of the Kootenays" initially consisted of tents and log cabins with dirt floors and sod roofs. The first hotel was a large tent, and lodgers ate their meals outdoors from a rough table. Most of Nelson's first settlers were Americans who mailed their letters with United States postage stamps and drank themselves into a stupor every July Fourth. As in most early mining camps, the painted ladies of the evening soon became well established. A halfway house stood between the mines and the town, and on payday the ladies went there to be closer to the miners and their money.

View of Nelson, British Columbia, 1898 — *Courtesy Provincial Archives, Victoria, British Columbia.*

Following a disastrous flood in 1894, Nelson recovered and took on a more permanent appearance. The Hall brothers sold their claims to a British syndicate for more than one million dollars. This made the Silver King Mine one of the first in the Kootenai region not controlled by American capital. The new company built a smelter in Nelson, along with a four-mile aerial ropeway from the mine to the smelter. In 1899, the town established the only electric street-car system between Vancouver and

General view of Kaslo, British Columbia — *Courtesy Provincial Archives, Victoria, British Columbia.*

Winnipeg. The two bright-red coaches ran throughout the business district until 1949. By the turn of the century, the visitor in Nelson could view elaborate homes full of gables, spires, turrets, and balustrated balconies. The huge, ornate opera house staged many exciting events before it went up in flames in 1935.

In the Slocan District, north of Nelson between Kootenay Lake and Arrow Lakes, prospectors discovered rich deposits of silver, lead, and zinc in the early 1890s. Among the first was the find of Eli Carpenter and John Seaton east of Slocan Lake. Their discovery set off a frantic silver rush. The town of Sandon west of Kootenay Lake soon had a population of two thousand. An equal number of people settled in Kaslo on the lake's western shore. Among the richest mines in "the silvery Slocan" were the Payne and the Slocan Star. Ore from this remote region came from the mines by wagon roads, tramways, and rawhide trails, which involved horses pulling sacks of ore down snow-covered hillsides. The Slocan boom ended with the worldwide decline in the price of silver in 1893. Several years later, the mines experienced a brief revival, only to have the best ore give out shortly after the turn of the century.

Southwest of Kootenay Lake near the south end of Arrow Lake, still another rich discovery came in the Trail Creek area where the LeRoi mines shipped ore south to be processed. The

Nelson, British Columbia's, first electric tram — *Courtesy Provincial Archives, Victoria, British Columbia.*

Opera house in Nelson, British Columbia — *Courtesy Provincial Archives, Victoria, British Columbia.*

61

Silversmith mine, Sandon, British Columbia, about 1900 — *Courtesy Provincial Archives, Victoria, British Columbia.*

Pack train, Sandon, British Columbia, 1904 — *Courtesy Provincial Archives, Victoria, British Columbia.*

town of Rossland grew to a population of six thousand. Along its Sourdough Alley, saloons entertained the miners twenty-four hours a day. To mill the LeRoi ore, mining magnate F. Augustus Heinze from Butte, Montana built a smelter in 1895 near the junction of Trail Creek and the Columbia River. He soon sold his interest to the Candian Pacific Railway, and the Trail smelter became the processing center for mines throughout the Kootenai Valley.

The large-scale mining which took place in the Kootenay Lake area had its parallel along the upper Kootenai. Here the first important developments did not begin until after 1890. During the 1880s, friction between Indians and whites occupied the attention of most of the people in the eastern valley.

Trouble arose with the influx of miners and settlers into the Indian ranges. When Kutenai Chief Isadore sought to prevent the whites from fencing the valley, the government intervened and placed the Indians on reservations. Serious problems arose in 1887 with the arrest of Kapula, a young Kutenai brave whom the whites accused of murdering two American prospectors three years earlier. Deeply aroused, Isadore and his tribesmen, armed with rifles, broke into the flimsy jail at Wild Horse and forced the constable to release Kapula. The Kutenai chief told the law enforcement officer to leave the district and announced that in the future any of his people charged with crime would be punished under tribal law.

The panic-stricken settlers sought government help. Assistance came in the form of seventy-five red-coated Northwest Mounted Police under the command of Colonel Sam Steele. The Colonel obtained the land at the confluence of Wild Horse Creek and the Kootenai River, where he erected Fort Steele. He then presided over the hearing of Kapula and his accused co-murderer Little Isadore, and dismissed the prisoners for lack of evidence. He concluded that the killings might well have been committed by white vagrants. Steele then settled the Indians' land grievances quickly and amiably; the Indians received more land for their reserves. Before the Mounties departed, after a stay of less than a year, Colonel Steele praised the behavior of the Kutenais. Chief Isadore promised that if future trouble arose his people would seek the counsel of their new friends, the Redcoats.

Much of the credit for this settlement belonged to Father Nicholas Coccola of St. Eugene's Misson. This Corsica-born

Sandon, British Columbia, 1896 — *Courtesy Provincial Archives, Victoria, British Columbia.*

Rossland, British Columbia, 1896 — *Courtesy Provincial Archives, Victoria, British Columbia.*

priest helped to persuade Chief Isadore to meet with Colonel Steele and to surrender Kapula and Little Isadore for the hearing. Later, Coccola opened a school for Indian children at the mission. He continued to spread the Christian Gospel and care for the sick in mining camps up and down the Kootenai Valley.

The population of the eastern valley increased rapidly early in the 1890s with the discovery of the North Star Mine by the French Canadian, Joe Bourgeois. A group of Kutenai Indians had found the ore while picking berries high in the mountains above Fort Steele. They then led Bourgeois and his party to the area. Subsequent removal of the ore required heavy machinery. The North Star Mining Company hacked out a twenty-one mile wagon

Colonel Sir Samuel B. Steele — *Courtesy Provincial Archives, Victoria, British Columbia.*

road, the McGinty Trail. Teams of mules hauled out ore at a rate of thirty tons a day to the Kootenai River, where boats took it south to be processed.

The North Star find touched off an influx of prospectors into the same region where others had rushed thirty years earlier. At Fort Steele, lots sold rapidly as stores, hotels, and saloons sprang up. A sawmill and brewing company began operations in the town. Tobacco Plains settlers watched many teams of horses heading north to Fort Steele daily.

Shortly after the discovery of the North Star, four American prospectors, Walter Burchette, Ed Smith, Pat Sullivan, and John Cleaver, crossed the Selkirk Range and found an entire mountain of lead-zinc ore which eventually became the famous Sullivan Mine. Early attempts to process the area's complex ore proved unprofitable even after the Spokane owners built a smelter five miles below the mine at Marysville. In 1909, they sold the mine to Canada's Consolidated Mining and Smelting Company for the low price of two hundred thousand dollars. Cominco developed a flotation process for handling the ore, and the Sullivan became one of North America's largest producers of lead and zinc.

Between the two branches of the Canadian Kootenai near

Smelter at Trail, British Columbia, 1896 — *Courtesy Provincial Archives, Victoria, British Columbia.*

Riverside Avenue, Fort Steele, British Columbia, 1898 — *Courtesy Provincial Archives, Victoria, British Columbia.*

Moyie Lake, a Kutenai Indian named Pierre discovered a rich body of galena ore. At St. Eugene's Mission, Father Coccola had often encouraged the Indians to search for the area's mineral wealth. The proceeds from the sale of the Moyie find enabled Coccola to build a new church at the mission. Pierre received a new cabin and a life-time annuity. With outside capital, the St. Eugene became the largest producer of lead in all of Canada. In ten years, it yielded more than eleven million dollars in ore and employed over four hundred men until the vein ran out in 1911.

The large-scale operations at mines such as the Sullivan and St. Eugene caused Canadian Kootenai metals production to increase steadily in value during the early twentieth century. By 1916, aided by wartime demand, the total value of the Kootenai district's metal products exceeded twelve million dollars; it had amounted to only a four million figure two decades earlier. In 1906, several Kootenai mining companies merged to form the Consolidated Mining and Smelting Company or Cominco. It was this concern which soon gained control of Sullivan Mine and the Trail smelter, and for the first time, Canadian capital became dominant in the Kootenai mines.

During these years of growth and prosperity along the Canadian Kootenai, the area of the loop also experienced a boom

St. Eugene mine buildings near Moyie, British Columbia — *Courtesy Provincial Archives, Victoria, British Columbia.*

which led to the first permanent settlement. By 1887, gold discoveries on the Vermillion River and Libby Creek, two tributaries of the Kootenai, created a small camp in the Libby area. A year later, James Stonechest, Robert Hulse, and Bart Downey opened the rich Banner and Bangle Mine near present Troy, Montana.

The town on lower Libby Creek grew rapidly and soon included fourteen saloons and numerous stores. Merchants freighted goods up the Bull Lake Road at a cost of ten dollars per hundred pounds. Two brickyards began operation — even though a rainstorm dissolved the first load of Kootenai clay bricks produced. Early Libby had its share of violence. On one occasion, a man known as "French Charley" struck and killed his woman with a plank, but no one pressed charges. Later, in response to a threat, Henry Van Wyck blew off French Charley's head with a shotgun. Van Wyck pleaded self-defense, was acquited, and later became the prominent justice of the peace who presided over Libby's first jury trial. In 1891, the survey for the Great Northern Railway passed to the north of Libby. This led virtually the entire town to move along the right-of-way near the southern bank of the Kootenai.

Above and Below: Front Street, Libby, Montana, before and after the July 1906 fire — *Courtesy Lincoln County Library, Libby, Montana.*

J.P. Wall store, Libby, Montana — *Courtesy Lincoln County Library, Libby, Montana.*

Hoffman's saloon, Libby, Montana — *Courtesy Lincoln County Library, Libby, Montana.*

Ore wagon from Snowshoe mine, Libby, Montana — *Courtesy Lincoln County Library, Libby, Montana.*

Mining car in the Libby area — *Courtesy Lincoln County Library, Libby, Montana.*

Development of the hard-rock mines on the Kootenai Loop required heavy machinery and big money. Some of the earliest mines near Libby included the Silver Crown, Granite Creek, and several mines on Fisher Creek. Sylvanite on the Yaak River also became an important mining area. But the mine which contributed more than any other to the growth of Libby was the Snowshoe, located sixteen miles south of the town. The mine's discoverers, John Abbott and A. F. Dunlap, named it after a broken snowshoe which had hindered their staking of the claim in the deep snow. The original owners leased the mine to outside investors who installed a compressor and shipped ore out in freight wagons. Later, a British firm bought the mine. The Snowshoe produced more than a million dollars in lead, silver, and gold before it fell into receivership in 1912.

In the early years of the twentieth century, mines on Granite Creek and Fisher Creek, along with logging and railroading, kept Libby growing. In 1916, Troy's Banner and Bangle Mine, renamed the Snowstorm, built a large concentrator and employed more than 150 men. A seven-mile electric railway ran between the mine and the mill.

With the formation of Lincoln County in 1910, Libby and the Tobacco Plains town of Eureka engaged in an intense rivalry for the county seat. Eureka won the close election, but the courts reversed the outcome in Libby's favor because of some irregular votes.

Much of the mining population throughout the Kootenai Valley was transient, but a few prospectors remained to begin farming and ranching. The number of farms in the Montana Kootenai Valley grew from twelve in 1892 to nearly three hundred in 1910. Homesteaders in the Libby and Troy area usually cleared a little land each year on which they raised wheat, vegetables, hay, small orchards, poultry, and livestock. Other homestead claimants were mere speculators who hoped to sell the timber from the land. The Great Northern Railway also engaged in farmland speculation. Around 1910, the Great Northern led a huge promotion scheme advertising the Kootenai Loop as a mecca for the growing of fruit. This drew many settlers into the valley, but the land proved unsuitable for large-scale fruit growing. Most of the fruit farmers changed to raising livestock or sought work as lumbermen.

At Tobacco Plains, the first white settlers were stockmen. The region boasted some of the best grazing land in the entire

Kootenai Valley. Ranches sprang up in the late 1860s as cattlemen brought in plows on pack horses. Most practiced open-range grazing throughout much of the year until the severe winter of 1892—1893 killed more than one-half of the area's livestock. From then on, stockmen started fencing land and raising hay. With the coming of the railroad, homesteaders began to fill the area, clearing and fencing off the 160 acres allotted to them by the federal government. After five years' residence and sufficient improvements, a settler secured free title to his section.

Early homesteaders found travel so difficult that they journeyed to town for supplies only once or twice each year. They

Drilling in a mine near Libby — *Courtesy Lincoln County Library, Libby, Montana.*

Buildings near the Snowshoe mine, Libby — *Courtesy Lincoln County Library, Libby, Montana.*

traveled by wagon or sleigh, padding the seats with quilts and using heated stones to keep their feet warm. They occasionally broke the monotony of months of isolation with all-night neighborhood dances. They gathered at local hotels or halls which often came furnished with bunks, which allowed children to sleep while parents danced.

North of the border, stockmen and farmers settled on land all along the river. A few took up sections on the upper Kootenai during the Wild Horse gold rush. Among the first landowners were Peter Fernie, Michael Phillips, Robert Mather, and Colonel James Baker. Baker bought land near Galbraith's ferry and named it Cranbrook after his birthplace in England. By 1890, the upper Kootenai supported thirty-nine farms. This number grew rapidly once the second mining rush got underway.

Along the lower Kootenai, farmers settled in the rich valleys around Bonners Ferry, Idaho, even though spring floods plagued them. Settlers raised hay, wheat, vegetables, and livestock near Kootenay Lake, and about 1900, O. J. Wegen began the area's commercial fruit industry.

Large-scale agriculture in the valley of Kootenay Lake would have developed far earlier had William A. Baillie-Grohman had his way. This world traveler and distant cousin of the Duke of Wellington arrived in the Kootenai country in 1882 while on a big game hunting expedition. He observed that the area where the Kootenai emptied into Kootenay Lake contained some of the richest soil in British Columbia, but every year the river flooded and rendered the land worthless for agriculture. While traveling near the upper Kootenai at the place David Thompson had called McGillivray's Portage, Baillie-Grohman noticed how the Kootenai flowed to within one mile of Columbia Lake, the headwaters of the Columbia River. Observing that the lake was lower in elevation than the Kootenai, the Englishman proposed

William A. Baillie-Grohman — *Courtesy Provincial Archives, Victoria, British Columbia.*

to dig a channel across McGillivray's Portage to divert the Kootenai into the Columbia. He reasoned that this would lower the river near Kootenay Lake and reclaim the valuable alluvial soil.

Baillie-Grohman negotiated with the British Columbia Government and gained a ten-year lease on the entire lower Kootenai Valley between the lake and the American boundary. He then obtained financial support from British investors and formed the Kootenay Lake Syndicate. His planning included a scheme to bring settlers into the reclaimed land.

Baillie-Grohman's Kootenai canal under construction — *Courtesy Provincial Archives, Victoria, British Columbia.*

When Baillie-Grohman had first conceived his project, very few settlers lived in the upper Columbia Valley, and so the diversion, which would raise the level of the Columbia substantially, would have harmed no one. But as he proceeded, the Canadian Pacific Railway's main line reached the upper Columbia, and with it, settlers began to arrive. The railway used its political influence to get the Canadian government to block the diversion plan. The government still allowed Baillie-Grohman to construct his canal, but he had to furnish it with a lock.

Lock on the Kootenai canal — *Courtesy Provincial Archives, Victoria, British Columbia.*

Moreover, he had to sign an agreement that the channel would not affect the volume of water in the Columbia or the Kootenai. This, of course, defeated the very purpose of the canal.

Baillie-Grohman went ahead and dug his ditch anyway, for he had deposited an indemnity with the government which would give him a sizable land grant only if he completed the canal. Later the British entrepreneur described the project as "a job I can honestly recommend to those desirous of committing suicide in a decent, gentlemanly manner." He established the settlement of Grohman in the region which became known as Canal Flats. The construction crew included Chinese, Swedes, French Canadians, and Indians.

After its 1889 completion, Baillie-Grohman's waterway measured 6,700 feet long and 45 feet wide with a 100-foot-long lock.

Recent view of Canal Flat showing the old canal in the foreground —
Courtesy Provincial Archives, Victoria, British Columbia.

Fear of flooding on the Columbia led the government to keep the canal closed, and it soon fell into disuse. The Englishman then began work to widen the outlet of Kootenay Lake in order to lower its level. He soon ran out of funds, and in 1892 he abandoned the Kootenai Valley forever, having spent a fortune without reclaiming a single acre of land. It was to be more than forty years before Baillie-Grohman's dream of rich harvests on reclaimed lower Kootenai bottomlands would become a reality.

6

The Age of Steam

Without railroads, the second mining boom in the Kootenai country would not have occurred. It was the railroads, aided by Kootenai River steamboats, which transported the heavy equipment necessary for hard-rock mining. It was the railroads which advertised the valley and attracted people and capital. It was the railroads which hauled the products of the mines, smelters, and farms to eastern and western markets.

Nature did not design the region to accommodate railway routes. The towering Rocky Mountains stood as formidable barriers. Beyond them lay the Rocky Mountain Trench, where the Columbia and Kootenai Rivers made great bends to avoid the Selkirk and Purcell Ranges. Geography largely determined that the first transcontinental rail lines in the American-Canadian border region would pass along the northern and southern edges of the Kootenai country.

Ever since the Wild Horse gold rush, the government of British Columbia had hoped to establish a solid communications link with the isolated Kootenai region. Gilbert Malcolm Sproat, commissioned by the provincial government to explore the area in 1884, warned that British Columbia would lose all of the Kootenai trade to the Americans unless she spent large sums to construct wagon roads and place steamboats on the river.

Canadians throughout the 1870s pressed for a transcontinental railroad. In 1880, a syndicate of Canadians and Americans led by James Jerome Hill financed the proposed Canadian Pacific Railroad, and construction soon began.

Canadian Pacific explorer Major A. B. Rogers — *Courtesy Provincial Archives, Victoria, British Columbia.*

Hill chose Major A. B. Rogers, a prairie surveyor who had never seen a mountain, to find a route through the Rockies and Selkirks. Rogers' diet consisted of beans and chewing tobacco, and he drove his men mercilessly. After more than a year of difficult exploration, during which he traveled most of the length of the Kootenai River, Rogers found a satisfactory pass. Once it was completed in 1885, the Canadian Pacific main line passed too far north of the Kootenai to serve the region well, but the Columbia River linked the Kootenai to the railway, making it the most accessible Canadian route into the area.

James J. Hill, meanwhile, had fallen out with the other officials of the Canadian Pacific after they had refused to build part of the railroad in the United States. He then planned and constructed his own Great Northern line to the Pacific which ran between the Canadian Pacific and the Northern Pacific. When he began to send feeder lines into Canada, the Canadian Pacific built branch lines to the south. The remote Kootenai country thus became a center of intense rivalry between American and Canadian railroads.

In 1889, Hill sent Charles R. B. Haskell and John F. Stevens west to survey a route through the divide to the Kootenai. Haskell and his party went down the Kootenai and up the Fisher River to Haskell Pass — the route which the main line of Hill's Great Northern Railway eventually followed. The tracks reached the Kootenai loop at Jennings, Montana, and followed the river

Canadian Pacific and Great Northern Railway magnate James J. Hill
— *Courtesy Montana Historical Society.*

west to Libby, which they reached in May 1892. Construction crews included many Greek, Italian, and Chinese immigrants. They laid the rails by hand and used steam drills and steam shovels to construct the grade. Bridge timbers had to be hand-hewn from local timber. Landslides were common, especially in Kootenai Canyon west of Libby. Many early railroaders lost their lives on this hazardous stretch.

The coming of the railroad led to the birth of numerous new towns along the route. Among these was Troy, Montana, located about twenty miles down the Kootenai from Libby. Great Northern surveyor E. L. Preston laid out the townsite and soon, as one early settler related, "fifteen saloons gaily lit were filled to the doors with wild men and wild women yelling, singing, dancing, and cursing with glasses lifted high." When the construction workers left, more permanent residents settled in Troy. A new Great Northern roundhouse provided many jobs. Early Troy had a reputation for lawlessness. During a railroad strike, someone robbed several boxcars filled with clothing and distributed it to needy residents. The local prosecuting attorney lamented, "if we convicted anybody, looks like we'd have to convict the whole damn town. . . ."

Annerly, the first steamboat on the upper Kootenai — *Courtesy Provincial Archives, Victoria, British Columbia.*

First Great Northern train to reach Libby, Montana — *Courtesy Lincoln County Library, Libby, Montana.*

Views of early Troy, Montana — *Courtesy Montana Historical Society.*

Other towns on the loop, such as Jennings and Bonners Ferry, flourished both because of the railroad traffic and the steamboats which began to ply the Kootenai regularly in the 1890s. Unlike most areas where railroads replaced the riverboats, the arrival of the steel rails gave Kootenai steamboating its first real impetus.

In 1882, Captain Francis Patrick Armstrong entered the Kootenai country as an explorer for the Canadian Pacific Railway. He decided to homestead on Columbia Lake and supply food to the railroad construction camps. To deliver potatoes at

Upper Kootenai steamboat *Gwendoline* – *Courtesy Provincial Archives, Victoria, British Columbia.*

Golden he built two bateaux and hired Indians to row them. With the railroad's completion came settlers who needed supplies, and so Armstrong replaced the slow bateaux with steam-powered boats. By 1888, he was shipping freight and passengers regularly on the upper Columbia. In 1891, he incorporated the Upper Columbia Navigation and Tramway Company. This corporation owned both steamboats and tramways, including a horse-drawn tram which crossed Canal Flats between Columbia Lake and the Kootenai.

The Great Northern Railway reached the Kootenai at about the same time that the North Star Mine opened. The nearest smelters at Great Falls, Montana, and Everett, Washington, lay on the

Upper Kootenai steamer *North Star* – *Courtesy Provincial Archives, Victoria, British Columbia.*

Upper Kootenai steamboat *J.D. Farrell* – *Courtesy Provincial Archives, Victoria, British Columbia.*

85

Great Northern line. Between the mine and the railhead at Jennings flowed 130 miles of navigable Kootenai River. Former Texas stockman B. Walter Jones and Captain Harry Depew recognized the opportunity and launched a small stern-wheeler, the *Annerly*, which became the first steamboat to navigate the upper Kootenai. A woman passenger described the *Annerly's* maiden voyage:

The prospectors cooked their meals over a sheet of tin on a coal stove in the middle of the boat. I ate at the Captain's table . . . The men slept on the floor; I slept in a curtained corner on a mattress. There were no cabins.

During the trip a cable used to pull the boat across narrow rapids broke, and the boat shot downstream, running aground on a sand bar. The passengers then clambered out while the crew pulled the boat up the rapids. After this hectic voyage, the *Annerly* made regular trips, hauling ore and passengers between Jennings and Fort Steele.

It was not long before the *Annerly* had competition on the Kootenai run. Captain Armstrong began building the *Gwendoline* on the Kootenai, but lack of labor and materials forced him to pull the hull across Canal Flats and float it north to Golden to complete it. He then secured funds from the provincial government to repair the damaged Grohman Canal. In May 1894, the *Gwendoline* became the first and only boat ever to travel south up the Columbia and down the Kootenai. Heavy flooding that same spring rendered the canal useless once more. Still, with its tramways, Armstrong's company could provide passage from Golden on the Columbia to Fort Steele on the Kootenai.

In 1895, the North Star Mine completed the McGinty Trail and began hauling ore from the mine to the river. The rival Canadian and American companies — Armstrong's Upper Columbia Navigation and Tramway Company and Jones' Upper Kootenai Navigation Company — both signed contracts to haul the ore. Armstrong hired skilled Portland shipbuilders to construct the *Ruth* at Libby. His company then offered continuous freight and passenger service from Golden to Jennings, a distance of three hundred miles.

B. W. Jones' American company also built a new stern-wheeler, the *Rustler*, but shortly after her launching, she struck a rock in Jennings Canyon. Fortunately, the *Annerly* arrived to

The *Midge,* first steamboat on the Kootenai — *Courtesy Provincial Archives, Victoria, British Columbia.*

Kootenay Lake steamboat *Galena – Courtesy Provincial Archives, Victoria, British Columbia.*

State of Idaho en route to Bonners Ferry — *Courtesy Provincial Archives, Victoria, British Columbia.*

rescue the *Rustler*'s passengers only minutes before the boat sank. Jones hired a professional diver from Chicago to search for the *Rustler*'s expensive boiler, but it was never found. Shortly after this disaster, the Upper Kootenai Navigation Company sold out to Armstrong, giving the Canadian a monopoly on eastern Kootenai passenger and freight service.

The treacherous waters of Jennings Canyon did not discriminate between Americans and Canadians. On May 7, 1897, the *Gwendoline* and the *Ruth*, both laden with North Star ore, entered the canyon. Suddenly, a log lodged in the *Ruth*'s paddlewheel, rendering the craft uncontrollable. She crashed against rocks on the shore, and passengers scrambled onto the bank for safety. The wreckage of the *Ruth* blocked the narrow channel for the oncoming *Gwendoline*. The boat struck the rocks and tore off much of her starboard side, but Armstrong managed to pilot her to safety.

A month later, the *Gwendoline* was repaired and a new 130-foot steamer, the *North Star*, joined her. Called by many the finest boat ever to ply the Kootenai, the *North Star* carried 100 passen-

The *Nelson* at Kaslo, British Columbia — *Courtesy Provincial Archives, Victoria, British Columbia.*

gers and 150 tons of freight. With the upper Kootenai mining rush at its peak, these two boats could not haul passengers and freight to the ore fields fast enough. In late 1897, American investors formed a rival firm, the Kootenai River Transportation Company, and launched the *J. D. Farrell* from Jennings. This modern stern-wheeler, complete with electric lights and steam heat, made its first trip too early in the season in low water and ran aground on nearly every sandbar between Jennings and Fort Steele.

In 1898, the Fort Steele boom ended, and the Canadian Pacific's branch line reached east Kootenai, enabling ore to be hauled by rail to the Trail smelter. These developments killed the trade of the Kootenai steamboats. By the following year, the *Gwendoline* and the *North Star* did not even operate. Then the *Gwendoline*, while being shipped by rail to Kootenay Lake, tumbled off a flatcar into the river and was totally wrecked.

Shortly after the turn of the century, upper Kootenai steamboating revived briefly when boats carried supplies and men to construction camps for the Great Northern's branch railway line

The *International* near Kaslo — *Courtesy Provincial Archives, Victoria, British Columbia.*

The *Kaslo* on Kootenay Lake — *Courtesy Provincial Archives, Victoria, British Columbia.*

to Fernie, British Columbia. After the railroad's completion, Captain Armstrong decided to run the *North Star* through the old Grohman canal to use her for ore trade on the upper Columbia. Because the ship was too large for the canal's locks, Armstrong replaced them with sandbag dams. After the water in the canal rose enough to float the vessel, dynamite exploded the second dam and the battered *North Star* chugged into Columbia Lake.

Steamer *Kokanee* at Nelson, British Columbia — *Courtesy Provincial Archives, Victoria, British Columbia.*

The boat experienced only limited success on the upper Columbia, and eventually Armstrong dismantled her. By 1915, the steamboating era on the upper Columbia had come to a close.

On the lower Kootenai and Kootenay Lake, the steamboat age began earlier and lasted longer. W.A. Baillie-Grohman launched the first steamer on Kootenay Lake in 1884 in connection with his land reclamation project. He had the small steamboat, the *Midge*, shipped from Europe where she had navigated the waters of the Norwegian Fjords. The Northern Pacific carried the boat to

Kootenay Lake steamer *Moyie* – *Courtesy Provincial Archives, Victoria, British Columbia.*

Sandpoint, Idaho. From there a crew of Indians and whites, aided by rollers and pulleys, moved the *Midge* forty miles overland to Bonners Ferry where she was launched. She became the first steamer to navigate the Kootenai River. Indians along Kootenay Lake cut wood for the boat's boiler in return for having their canoes towed by the little steamer.

With the opening of the Hall Mines near Nelson in 1888, Richard Fry of Bonners Ferry bought the steam tug *Idaho* which he hauled from Sandpoint. He used the boat to transport ore from the Kootenay Lake mines to Bonners Ferry. In that same year, the Kootenai Mining and Smelting Company launched the screw propeller steamer *Galena* — the first passenger boat on Kootenay Lake.

During the early 1890s, the Canadian Pacific and Great Northern Railways both extended lines into the Kootenay Lake region. They also engaged in intense competition for the lake steamship trade throughout the decade. Nakusp became the Canadian Pacific port, while Kaslo served as Great Northern's base.

In 1890, encouraged by the Canadian Pacific, a number of

steamboat owners joined to form the Columbia and Kootenay Steam Navigation Company. The firm soon had two boats, the *Kootenai* and the *Lytton*, plying the Columbia and the Kootenai. The company then launched the *Nelson*, the first sternwheeler on Kootenay Lake. This large steamer carried supplies to lake centers and up the river to Bonners Ferry. She sought to divert trade to Nelson where it could employ Canadian Pacific rail connections.

American competition on Kootenay Lake began in 1892, when the Great Northern Railway formed the Kootenai Railway and Navigation Company. By the following year, the company owned the tug *Kaslo*, numerous barges, and the new sternwheeler, *State of Idaho*. Throughout the summer of 1893, the *Nelson* and the *State of Idaho* engaged in a fierce contest for the lake trade. The faster *State of Idaho* succeeded in diverting much of the freight traffic to the Great Northern's Bonners Ferry terminal until the ship ran ashore and crashed in a fog.

The riverboat traffic on the lower Kootenai led to the rapid growth of Bonners Ferry, Idaho. In 1893, the town officially formed, and it soon became the county seat. Many of Bonners

Construction on the Crowsnest line — *Courtesy Provincial Archives, Victoria, British Columbia.*

Building a trestle on the Crowsnest line — *Courtesy Provincial Archives, Victoria, British Columbia.*

Canadian Pacific engine at Nelson, British Columbia — *Courtesy Provincial Archives, Victoria, British Columbia.*

Cranbrook, British Columbia, in 1904 — *Courtesy Provincial Archives, Victoria, British Columbia.*

Ferry's first buildings were perched on stilts, and during high water the Kootenai flowed beneath them. The town survived serious floods in 1894 and 1904. During the second deluge, residents shopped by walking on planks that were supported by beer kegs.

In 1896, the Columbia and Kootenay Steam Navigation Company launched the large passenger steamer, the *Kokanee*. Later that year, the Canadian Pacific bought out the entire company which then owned seven steamers and ten barges. The Great Northern's new ship, the *International*, soon challenged the *Kokanee* for the lake trade. This time the Canadian ship won the races across Kootenay Lake. Near the turn of the century, the Canadian Pacific gradually enlarged its lake fleet to include the steel stern-wheeler, the *Moyie*, and several powerful steam tugs which pulled barges.

Kootenay Lake passenger boats rivaled any of the "floating palaces" on eastern rivers. They contained drawing rooms complete with pianos, overstuffed furniture, and potted palms. They served the best meals on spotless tables set with ornate silver. Below decks, however, crews lived and worked in cramped, filthy conditions, and in the summer, the heat was nearly unbearable. Strong deck hands leaped from slippery gangplanks to wharves to tie the boats and begin unloading the heavy cargo.

Steamers continued to serve the towns along Kootenay Lake through the first half of the Twentieth Century. In 1931, they received a serious blow with the completion of a rail link around the southern end of the lake. The last of the stern-wheelers, the *Moyie*, was retired in 1957. Mounted on blocks at Kaslo, she remains a tourist attraction as a museum.

The competitive construction of Canadian Pacific and Great Northern Branch lines ended steamboat trade on the Kootenai and linked the entire region to the rest of the United States and Canada. In 1890, Hill's Great Northern reached the Columbia in Canada with the Spokane Falls and Northern Railway. At the same time, the Canadian Pacific joined Robson, near the junction of the Kootenai and the Columbia, to the Kootenay Lake towns of Nelson and Procter.

In 1895, the Great Northern obtained the Nelson and Fort Shepherd line, which ran from Nelson to the American border. This connection gave Nelson and Kootenay Lake rail access to Spokane and the entire American rail system. Hill then gained control of a line between Slocan in the booming silver district and Kaslo on Kootenay Lake. This enabled the Great Northern to haul ore by rail and boat from Slocan to Bonners Ferry and the mills along the railway's main line. Another American entrepreneur, F.A. Heinze, built rail links from his smelter at Trail to the mines in the area.

The Canadian Pacific Railway officials recognized that they would have to act fast to end this massive diversion of Kootenai wealth to the United States on American rails. In 1897, the signing of the Crowsnest Pass Agreement gave the Canadian Pacific a government subsidy and sizable land grants for building a railroad from Lethbridge, Alberta, to Nelson.

Construction of the Crowsnest Railway employed five thousand men under the supervision of M.J. Haney, who finished the project in fifteen months. The workers labored under highly adverse conditions. The contracting companies often paid workers less than promised and charged them fees for services not provided. Illness ran rampant in the unsanitary construction camps where men crowded into unventilated bunkhouses. At one camp, a typhoid epidemic claimed over ninety lives. A small hospital erected at St. Eugene's Mission provided care for many of the victims of disease.

In October 1898, the line reached Kootenay Landing on the lake's eastern shore. The Canadian Pacific then built a rail link on

Fernie, British Columbia, following the 1908 fire — *Courtesy Provincial Archives, Victoria, British Columbia.*

The rebuilding of Fernie after the 1908 fire — *Courtesy Provincial Archives, Victoria, British Columbia.*

Great Northern Railway survey crew in northern Lincoln County, Montana — *Courtesy Lincoln County Library, Libby, Montana.*

the west shore between Procter and Nelson. Barges carried freight across the lake until 1931 when a route connected Procter to Kootenay Landing.

By crossing through Crowsnest Pass east of the Kootenai, the new railway ran through one of the richest coal deposits in North America. The town of Fernie on the railroad grew rapidly. Feeder lines brought in coal from the region's mines, and huge ovens produced coke for the west Kootenai smelters. A popular legend told of a Kutenai woman who had put a curse on the Fernie region because the town's founder, William Fernie, had refused to marry her. In its early years, the town certainly seemed cursed. In 1902, a mine explosion killed 127 men; three years later, a series of strikes tied up the mines for months; and in 1908, a brushfire consumed most of the town, leaving three thousand people homeless. Yet Fernie survived and grew.

Fort Steele promoters had labored long and hard to get the Crowsnest Railroad to pass through their town. At the same time, Colonel James Baker offered the railroad company shares in a proposed townsite at his Cranbrook estate. The line therefore

Laying Great Northern rails in Tobacco Valley, Montana — *Courtesy Lincoln County Library, Libby, Montana.*

bypassed Fort Steele and ran across Baker's homestead. In 1897, surveyors laid out a town at Cranbrook, and the railroad soon made the place a prosperous divisional point. After that, Fort Steele's wealth and population declined rapidly.

Shortly after completion of the Crowsnest Railway, the Canadian Pacific built a branch line from Cranbrook to Kimberley. This enabled it to ship ore from the Sullivan Mine to the Trail smelter. The Canadian Pacific purchased the smelter and all of F.A. Heinze's rail lines in the area in 1898.

James J. Hill did not remain an idle observer during these years. In 1898, his Great Northern constructed a line from Bonners Ferry to Kuskanook on the southern tip of Kootenay Lake. Three years later, after gaining control of the Crows Nest Coal Company, Hill began a branch line up the eastern Kootenai to Fernie. Railway towns such as Gateway, Newgate, and Rexford arose along this route. The Tobacco Plains town of Eureka, originally known as Deweyville, also grew rapidly once trains began arriving there regularly in 1904. Eureka survived a devastating fire to become an important lumber and commercial center.

Early Eureka, Montana — *Courtesy Montana Historical Society.*

Warland, Montana — *Courtesy Lincoln County Library, Libby, Montana.*

Early view of Bonners Ferry, Idaho — *Courtesy Mrs. Inez Herrig, Libby, Montana.*

Kootenai bridge at Bonners Ferry, Idaho — *Courtesy Idaho State Historical Society.*

Throughout the early Twentieth Century, the Great Northern continued to pull much of the traffic from the Canadian Kootenai into the United States.

In 1915, the Kootenay Central Railway linked the main Canadian Pacific line at Golden with the Crowsnest Railway. One year later, the Canadian Pacific purchased a railroad from Daniel C. Corbin which ran from Spokane through Bonners Ferry to the Crowsnest Line near Eastport, Idaho. This enabled the Canadian Pacific to provide the fastest rail service between the state of Washington and Chicago. The Crowsnest line through the Kootenai country became an important part of this transcontinental route. Each summer, as many as three trains daily rushed northwestern agricultural goods to eastern markets.

The many American and Canadian branch lines which ran throughout the Kootenai River region made it possible to ship bulky commodities to distant points. With rail access to markets both east and west, the wood products industry began to develop on a large scale all along the Kootenai.

7

Timber

Nearly every explorer and trader who traveled up and down the Kootenai River commented on the thick forests covering the countryside and the potential wealth they represented. But, as David Thompson recorded, the region's remoteness left its timber, "without a possibility of being brought to market." The first pioneers to enter the area sought other riches, and, except where a homesteader cleared his land or a prospector felled trees to build a cabin, they left the forests virtually untouched.

The coming of the railroads brought a sudden rise in the demand for timber. When railway construction began, many independent operators known as tie hacks cut the wood for the road beds. Skilled Scandinavians, using only axes, could turn out forty to sixty ties per day. Later, lumbermen brought in two-man whipsaws and began cutting boards.

Michael Phillips built the first sawmill in the Kootenai Valley along the river's eastern branch in Canada. This water-powered operation supplied lumber for miners at Wild Horse in the 1860s. Twenty years later, the industrious Englishman, Baillie-Grohman, ran a sawmill at Canal Flats which produced the timber for the lock in his canal. Baillie-Grohman gave the first board from his mill to an Indian woman who used it for a papoose carrying board. Later, lumber from this mill built coffins for Mounted Police who died in a typhoid epidemic at Fort Steele.

The first sawmill on the American side of the boundary came in 1889 when Tom Flowers and Charles Therriault brought a

The sawmill at Grohman, British Columbia — *Courtesy Provincial Archives, Victoria, British Columbia.*

large turbine, piece by piece, into Tobacco Plains on pack horses. They sent some of the lumber from their mill down the Kootenai on rafts to Jennings. The Libby townsite company erected that town's first sawmill after bringing in the machinery by wagon. This mill ran successfully for several years until one day when workmen overheated the boiler. It exploded, leaving everyone stunned but uninjured.

With the construction of the Crowsnest Railway and the many Great Northern branch lines, sawmills sprang up all along the Kootenai. Michigan lumberman Archie Leitch established a mill near Cranbrook, where the North Star Mill also began to operate. The East Kootenay Lumber Company near Cranbrook was the first to use a planer. One of the area's largest mills, the Cranbrook Lumber Company, employed more than sixty men.

Farther down the river, John Brenkenridge and Peter Lund built a mill at Wardner which later was run by the Crowsnest Lumber Company. By 1910, this mill had become the largest lumber operation in Canada's Kootenai country. Dozens of other mills consumed lots between Crowsnest Pass and Kootenay

Landing. Many more sprang up around Kootenay Lake, one of the first being located at Kaslo. At the mouth of the Kootenai, Waldie and Sons established a large mill near Castlegar.

As with the mining industry, American capital created the wood products boom in Canada's Kootenai country. Around the turn of the century, American lumbermen, having denuded eastern woodlands, staked easily secured claims to the Kootenai's lush forests. By 1910, Americans controlled ninety percent of all investments in the timberlands of British Columbia, and their mills turned out millions of board feet of lumber annually.

With the increase of lumbering and because many settlers were clearing wooded areas, the governments of both the United States and Canada set aside forest reserves and recruited rangers to manage them. As early as 1888, the Canadian Government began to establish reserves in British Columbia; some of the first were located in the Selkirk Mountains. The 1912 Forest Act created the British Columbia Forest Service and made it responsible for management of the province's forest resources. Not

Artist's depiction of rolling logs into a river canyon — *Courtesy Montana Historical Society.*

until the post-World War II era did the government pass strict legislation to regulate logging and control the indiscriminate rape of the region's timber lands.

The American government withdrew the first public land for forest reserves in 1891. An 1897 presidential proclamation set aside much of the Kootenai drainage forest which became known as the Lewis and Clark Reserve, Northern Division. In 1906, the Kootenai National Forest was created. Its borders have changed periodically until the establishment of its present boundaries in 1973. In 1908, Idaho's Kaniksu National Forest

Logging pole road — *Courtesy Montana Historical Society.*

came to include most of the Kootenai Valley within that state.

The first Civil Service examinations for forest rangers in 1905 required applicants to be "thoroughly sound and able bodied, capable of enduring hardships and performing severe labor under trying conditions." The earliest Kootenai rangers patrolled huge areas, fought forest fires, and constructed trails. They wore no distinguishing uniforms, and their equipment consisted of an ax, a gun, and a saddle horse. A ranger constructed his own headquarters — usually a small log cabin with a dirt floor.

Donkey engine and crew near Libby, Montana — *Courtesy St. Regis Paper Company, Libby, Montana.*

American and Canadian forest rangers met their toughest test in August of 1910, when a series of large forest fires blown by heavy winds destroyed more than three million acres in a forty-eight hour period. Hundreds of soldiers, rangers, and volunteers fought the blaze, which raged across much of the Pacific Northwest. Eighty-five men lost their lives. In the Kootenai region, the holocaust was less severe than in the area toward the south, but it razed many ranches and threatened to consume both Libby and Troy before being brought under control. In Canada, the most tragic of the 1910 fires occurred west of Kootenay Lake where four men became trapped and perished in a blaze.

The 1910 fire destroyed millions of dollars in timber, but the Kootenai logging industry survived and grew. By the turn of the century, the crosscut saw had replaced the ax as the tool for felling trees. Methods of hauling the logs from the forests also became more sophisticated. At first, horses skidded the logs and pulled the drays, sledges, and sleighs which hauled timber from the woods. Thus, most logging took place in the winter when snow slick for runners packed the forest floor. In some places, horses pulled flanged wheel trucks along wooden pole roads.

Early logging tractor — *Courtesy Montana Historical Society.*

Then, around 1900, the first logging railroads appeared. Shay locomotives equiped with special devices to keep wheels on the rough tracks hauled up to twenty-four carloads of lumber at once.

With the arrival of the railroads, donkey engines came into wide use. Loggers set these steam-powered drum winches near railroad tracks where their cables pulled in full-length trees. Horses then returned the cables to gather more felled trees. An eleven-man donkey crew could skid five carloads of logs or 80,000 board feet of timber each day. Later the more efficient Clyde skidder replaced the donkey engine.

Early logging camps were of two kinds — a string of railroad cars in which families lived with the men, and wooden shanties built near a donkey engine. Conditions in these camps were often deplorable. Ticks, lice, and bedbugs were common. Eating and sleeping facilities were filthy. In British Columbia, bunks were stacked four tiers high and were "muzzle-loaded" as weary loggers crawled into bed through the end of the bunk. Not until a 1917 strike did American lumberjacks even obtain real beds in their bunkhouses. Loggers worked as much as fifteen hours a day for very low wages. Most were transients, rough and hard on the outside, but full of compassion, especially when injury struck a fellow worker. Since most of the Scandinavian timber workers could not read English, they spent what little spare time they had in gambling.

Each spring many of these men participated in the huge log drives down the Kootenai River. For many years, beginning in 1899, most logs cut in the upper Kootenai drainage and along the Montana loop floated to mills downstream. The earliest drives went all the way to Kootenay Lake where boats towed the logs to mills at Nelson and Kaslo. Then in 1900, a group of men determined to keep American timber out of Canada built the Stein Lumber Company mill at Bonners Ferry and bought huge stands of timber from the homesteaders up the Kootenai. This firm soon became the Bonners Ferry Lumber Company run by Wisconsin merchant Frederick Weyerhaeuser.

Baird-Harper sawmill, Warland, Montana — *Courtesy Lincoln County Library, Libby, Montana.*

Dawson Lumber Company in Libby, Montana, about 1906 — *Courtesy Lincoln County Library, Libby, Montana.*

Settlers clearing their land hauled the logs to landings near the river where they awaited the spring drives. The logs which could not be rolled into the river went down specially built chutes. Some of these were five miles long and consisted of logs fastened together to form a trough. Many logs reached the Kootenai via tributary streams from Gold Creek and Elk River in British Columbia to Pipe Creek and Yaak River in Montana. The flood waters of the Kootenai were deep enough to avert any serious jams. On the smaller tributary streams, jams often took days to break free as drivers leaped from log to log in the icy water using dynamite and poles to release the logs.

Each drive involved millions of feet of larch, Douglas fir, and Ponderosa pine and stretched for miles along the Kootenai. The men of the driving crew wore spike shoes and carried peavies and poles. When not prodding logs, they traveled in long, slender bateaux. They ate meals in the cook's wanegan boat which followed the drives and carried the supplies. They portaged these boats around Kootenai Falls on railroad push cars while the logs shot over the falls. Despite obvious dangers, relatively few men lost their lives during the drives. Probably more injuries occurred after the drives when the lumbermen went into town to do their drinking, gambling, and fighting.

The annual log drives continued for only about ten years. Once the Montana legislature ruled that Montana cut timber had to be milled in the state and Canadian authorities prohibited transportation of logs across the border, the great Kootenai timber drives came to a halt.

Other problems plagued the Bonners Ferry Lumber Company. Spring floods often damaged facilities, and in 1909, the mill burned to the ground. Low market prices and high freight rates kept profits down. The mill finally closed for good in 1926. Other area mills continued to operate, and lumbering remained important to the Bonners Ferry economy.

In Montana, once timber no longer floated down the Kootenai to Idaho, local mills grew and prospered. At Tobacco Plains, the Eureka Lumber Company employed up to 300 men by 1915. In Libby, the Dawsons of Wisconsin built a large mill in 1906.

Eureka Lumber Company mill and Eureka, Montana, 1923 — *Courtesy University of Montana Library Archives, Missoula.*

Brydges and Fisher lumber mill, Nelson, British Columbia — *Courtesy Provincial Archives, Victoria, British Columbia.*

Peter Gerelle and Company mill at Nakusp, British Columbia — *Courtesy Provincial Archives, Victoria, British Columbia.*

Following the 1910 fire, another Wisconsin lumberman, Julius Neils, purchased the mill, and the J. Neils Lumber Company eventually became the largest single operation in all of Montana. In smaller Kootenai towns, such as Troy, Warland, and Jennings, lumber mills supported many families and kept the woods alive with activity. By 1912, the editor of Libby's *Western News* conceded that "without question, lumbering is Lincoln County's greatest industry and will continue to be so."

With the outbreak of World War I and the increased demand for lumber it created, the Kootenai mills produced at record levels. The war years also brought labor unrest. In April 1917, the Industrial Workers of the World, or "wobblies" as they were more commonly known, began a large strike which threatened to close down the huge Eureka Lumber Company mill. Fearing possible violence, merchants formed an Industrial Protective Association, and a hundred and fifty federal troops were sent to Eureka. To the south, the "wobblies" instigated strikes in Libby, Troy, and other northwestern Montana lumber camps. The walkouts ended in failure; the leaders were arrested and charged with sabotaging the war effort. The strikes did lead many owners to recognize the poor working conditions in the lumber industry, and they corrected some of the worst abuses. A 1919 Eureka strike to try to get an eight-hour day also failed, but several years later, the company did shorten the work day to eight hours.

In Canada's Kootenai country, lumbering grew as the economic mainstay throughout the early Twentieth Century. In many places, such as the Fernie region, American lumbermen invested heavily in sawmills and timberlands. Near the Moyie River the Lumberton mill stood for many years as one of the largest producers in the British Columbia interior. Wisconsin capitalists controlled this operation, which included a nineteen-mile flume — the second longest in North America. At its peak the Lumberton mill cut 150,000 feet of lumber daily. Mill workers lived in Cranbrook where they spent most of the company's $50,000 monthly payroll.

During the twenties and thirties, the Kootenai lumber industry followed the national business cycles of the United States and Canada. After a brief postwar lull, the 1920s witnessed increased profits and production, although many smaller mills closed down. In British Columbia, the timber industry became highly dependent on foreign sales. This made the depression of the

Crow's Nest Pass Lumber Company, Wardner, British Columbia, 1910 — *Courtesy Provincial Archives, Victoria, British Columbia.*

Lumberton, British Columbia, sawmill near Moyie Lake — *Courtesy Provincial Archives, Victoria, British Columbia.*

Bonners Ferry Lumber Company mill circa 1910 — *Courtesy Idaho State Historical Society.*

1930s even more severe when these markets disappeared. By 1932, the price of Ponderosa pine stood at one-half the 1929 level. As late as 1937, the Libby mill cut down its operating schedule to two days a week. The depression helped lead to the unionization of lumber workers both north and south of the international border. In 1931, the Lumber and Sawmill Union began organizing in British Columbia. Company owners resorted to every means of intimidation available to them, from firing of union organizers to blacklists, but they could not prevent Canadian timbermen from unionizing. In 1934 on the American side, the Lumber and Timber Union held the first Labor Day celebration ever observed in Libby. Wartime orders in the early forties ended the lumber slump in the Kootenai Valley. The problem which plagued the industry during the war was shortage of labor.

The years between the wars also brought technological innovations in the Kootenai lumber industry. By the mid-1930s, bulldozers were large enough to build roads into the roughly timbered mountains. Trucks then replaced Shay locomotives in the woods. The first logging trucks had topless cabs and solid rubber tires. Loads were often cinched down with chains, and so

J. Neils Loggers near Libby, 1930 — *Courtesy University of Montana Library Archives.*

when the logs rolled, they took the cab and driver with them. Gasoline-powered saws soon became the main method of felling trees.

Prior to World War II, many companies had exchanged clearcut lands for forest service timber. Beginning in the 1940s, the lumber industry in Montana, Idaho, and British Columbia began sustained yield logging. Though clear-cutting persisted, sustained yield practices grew more widespread and helped to insure the permanence of both the forests and the lumber industry.

In the last two decades, lumbering in the Kootenai Valley has become a diversified industry in which virtually every part of the tree is used. Pulp, paper products, treated posts and poles, compressed sawdust logs, plywood, and doors are just some of the products now manufactured in the region. In Montana, the Neils Mill continues to dominate the industry along the Kootenai. In 1955, Neils constructed a new mill and power plant at Troy. Two years later, the company merged with St. Regis Paper Company and built a new plywood plant in Libby. The St. Regis Company's entry into the Montana Kootenai country con-

J. Neils Lumber Company skidding logs near Libby, 1928 — *Courtesy U.S. Forest Service.*

tinued the tradition of outside capital dominating much of the valley's large-scale industry. Nation-wide St. Regis in 1976 ranked among the top one hundred and fifty industrial corporations in the United States, with assets totaling 1.4 billion dollars. Timber remained northern Idaho's chief industry after the war. Today five large mills, including the plants of Georgia Pacific and the Bonners Ferry Lumber Company, operate in Idaho's Kootenai Valley.

In Canada, several big forest-products companies currently dominate the Kootenai industry. Crestbrook Forest Industries employs more than a thousand men in sawmills at Creston and Cranbrook and at a modern pulp mill at Skookumchuk north of Kimberley. Nelson's main industry is Kootenay Forest Products Ltd., which operates a sawmill and plywood plant. In Castelgar at the river's mouth, over three hundred men work in the pulp and sawmill operations of the Celgar Company. Other smaller mills operate along the entire valley. The trees, once nagging obstacles to early pioneers, have become a permanent source of wealth for both the region and a vast outside market.

8

The Modern Era

The Kootenai country, like nearly every other area of Canada and the United States, experienced a revolution in transportation during the Twentieth Century. This revolution brought innovations to already existent industries, such as lumbering, and created at least one important new industry — tourism.

The automobile and the airplane came to the Kootenai Valley early in the century. Until 1912, no one had ever seen an airplane in the skies over the river. In the autumn of that year, the Nelson County Fair hired W.M. Stark to put on an air show over the town. Walter Edwards flew the sixty-horsepower Curtiss biplane on three short demonstrations. During the last flight, a sudden gust blew the plane away from the landing site, and horrified viewers watched it hit a fence. Neither plane nor pilot suffered serious damage. Similar air shows took place during the following decade in Kootenai towns on both sides of the boundary.

In August of 1919, Captain Ernest C. Hoy, flying a Curtiss Jenny, attempted the first flight across the Canadian Rockies. The pilot left Vancouver before sunrise, flew over Nelson, and reached Cranbrook at 2:05 P.M., where he landed on an open prairie. The town gave him a rousing welcome. He cleared the divide and landed at Lethbridge, Alberta, early that evening. His return flight to Vancouver followed a more northerly course over the upper Columbia. At Golden, he swerved on take-off to avoid hitting spectators, and he wrecked his plane.

On the same day as Hoy's historic flight, Lieutenant E.O. Hall also attempted to fly across the Rockies near the international border. Hall passed over Nelson shortly before Hoy did, but a fuel shortage forced him to land at a lumber mill near Creston. While trying to take off, he crashed into a parked automobile.

These pioneers of Kootenai aviation opened a new era which brought the gradual growth of airports from graded fields to modern paved runways and terminal facilities. During the great depression, unemployed workers of the Civilian Conservation Corps constructed runways at both Libby and Troy. Today Nel-

Captain Ernest C. Hoy at the beginning of his historic flight —
Courtesy Provincial Archives, Victoria, British Columbia.

son and Kaslo have amphibious air harbors on Kootenay Lake. Several small regional airlines link the area's towns, and Pacific Western Airline serves the cities of the Canadian Kootenai. On February 11, 1978 the Cranbrook airport became the scene of one of the worst air disasters in Canadian history. While attempting to land in a snowstorm, a Pacific Western jet overshot the runway killing forty of the plane's forty-seven passengers.

Modern highways also tie these towns together today, but the first automobile drivers had no such conveniences. To these

Pilot E.O. Hall in his airplane — *Courtesy Provincial Archives, Victoria, British Columbia.*

pioneers, roads were poor trails, and filling stations did not exist. The first car in Nelson had to confine itself to city streets, because only the railroad and narrow horse trails joined the Queen City to the outside world. Nils Hanson brought the first automobile, a 1906 Rambler, into the east Kootenai region. The car chased horses from the road and drew stares from everyone it passed.

In the loop country, Frank Stoop of Kalispell made the first automobile trip to Libby on a road which followed an abandoned railroad grade. Soon several men in Libby owned cars. By 1915, a road linked Libby and Troy through treacherous canyon country. The route was part of the Great National Parks Auto Highway, and it soon brought many tourists into the area.

Shortly after the road's completion, Frank Stoop, driving a Hudson, set a record which the press predicted would last a long time. He drove from Kalispell to Spokane in ten hours and fifty minutes, averaging more than twenty-five miles per hour. West of Troy, the car blew out a plug into the water system; Stoop replaced it with a whittled stick. Between the Yaak River and Moyie Springs, two stops were necessary — one to cut a large tamarack tree from the road and another to put on chains to get the car out of a mudhole.

First auto on Canada's Banff-Windermere road — *Courtesy Provincial Archives, Victoria, British Columbia.*

First automobiles in Nelson, British Columbia — *Courtesy Provincial Archives, Victoria, British Columbia.*

Mrs. T. M. Kennedy, the first lady to cross Kootenai bridge at Libby — *Courtesy Lincoln County Library, Libby, Montana.*

An asset of Lincoln County's first roads were the modern bridges across the Kootenai. Crews constructed these bridges in Libby, Troy, and Rexford after a 1910 ferry accident in Libby had taken five lives. In 1924, a road connected Libby with Rexford and united all of Lincoln County with highways.

In Canada, the upper Kootenai became accessible by highway around 1910. In 1913, Thomas W. Wilby traversed the Kootenai country as part of the first motor trip across Canada from coast to coast. Wilby reached the river near Wardner after coming through Crows Nest Pass. At Cranbrook, residents advised the motorist against attempting to cross the narrow mountain trail between the eastern Kootenai and Kootenay Lake. Wilby ig-

Early automobilers, Libby, Montana — *Courtesy Montana Historical Society.*

nored the warnings and proceeded to Creston on a road "narrow and strewn with boulders." At times his car sank to its hubs in mud. Near Yahk the road ended, so Wilby drove along the railroad bed, nervously aware that at any moment an approaching train might put an abrupt end to his travels. Finally Wilby's car reached Creston, becoming the first automobile ever to enter that town by road.

Another early motor road, the Banff-Windermere route, crossed the Canadian Rockies and went through Vermillion Pass, down the Kootenai Valley, and over Sinclair Pass to the upper Columbia. Later, improved highways linked the southern Kootenai Valley with the eastern provinces, and by 1940, the eastern Kootenai contained more than 1,800 miles of roads, and the Kootenay Lake region had over 1,100 miles. With the 1964

First truck of the Libby Volunteer Fire Department — *Courtesy Lincoln County Library, Libby, Montana.*

completion of a route east of Creston across 5,800-foot Kootenay Pass, the region could claim Canada's highest major highway.

With the highways came the tourist trade. The Kootenai country had always possessed some of the best climate, scenery, fishing and hunting in North America, but the lack of good roads had closed it to all but a few. The completion of the Banff-Windermere route brought the establishment of Kootenay National Park at the river's headwaters. Following World War II, the Park underwent a vast construction of new facilities. For the first time, the road became open all year long.

To the south and on Kootenay Lake, tourism has grown rapidly in recent years. Each summer the area attracts thousands of fishermen and campers. Fort Steele, which had degenerated to a near ghost town, has become a historic site. The buildings of the fort and town have been restored, and the government has built many new facilities, including a large, attractive museum and a theatre where plays entertain large audiences throughout the summer. Near Creston, the provincial government recently set aside one of Canada's largest waterfowl preservation areas. Winter sports have become big business in the Canadian Kootenai. The larger cities have built ice hockey arenas, and Kimberley and Fernie both contain growing ski areas with modern accommodations.

In the loop, Eureka, Libby, and Bonners Ferry widely advertise the excellent fishing, hunting, and skiing in the Kootenai and surrounding valleys. The recent completion of Libby Dam

Two early scenes from Kootenay National Park, British Columbia — *Courtesy Provincial Archives, Victoria, British Columbia.*

125

promises to attract large numbers of tourists each year to the camping and boating facilities along Lake Koocanusa.

In addition to the tourist trade, mining and agriculture have remained vital to the economy along the Kootenai. During the twenties and thirties, numerous mines and small mills operated sporadically in the Montana and Idaho Kootenai region. From Idaho, the International Molybdenum Company shipped ore to Spokane. Another company ran a large placer operation on Boulder Creek near the Montana border. Tributaries of the Kootenai in Montana, such as Rainy Creek, Granite Creek, and West Fisher Creek, were scenes of mining activity between the world

Kootenai bridge and boat landing, Fort Steele, British Columbia —
Courtesy Provincial Archives, Victoria, British Columbia.

wars. In 1933 at the height of the depression, the *Western News* of Libby could still report that six ore mills operated in Lincoln County. During the 1930s, scores of unemployed men searched the hills and washed the gravel of the streams for gold in order to pay their living expenses until economic conditions improved.

The mining discovery near the Montana Kootenai which proved to be of most lasting duration was the find of a coal-like mineral known as vermiculite. E.N. Alley, who developed the substance in the early 1920s, experimented and determined its value as an insulator, fire-proof roofing material, and an ingredient in paint and wallboard. By the 1930s, the Zonolite Com-

Vermiculite storage and loading facilities, Libby, Montana —
Courtesy W. R. Grace and Company.

pany was mining tons of vermiculite and shipping most of it to eastern areas to be processed. The Zonolite mine on Rainy Creek became one of the main employers in the Libby Area. In 1971, the owners of the mine, W.R. Grace Company, constructed a seven million dollar mill, blender, and storage facility.

In Canada, a vast development of water power and improved smelting processes in the 1920s led to a huge increase in the output of non-ferrous metals. The value of all metals produced in the Canadian Kootenai Valley increased from 5.4 million dollars in 1921 to 27.6 million dollars in 1929. The depression dealt a serious setback to this industry, as the 1931 output was less than one-half that of 1929.

Since the 1920s, the Consolidated Mining and Smelting Company has dominated the metals industry in southeastern British Columbia. Cominco's Sullivan Mine at Kimberley has produced more than 108 million tons of ore to be processed at the world's largest lead-zinc smelter in Trail. The Sullivan Mine today employs more than one thousand men in its over 150 miles of tunnels and huge underground crushing chamber. In 1966, the Cominco complex at Kimberley began producing steel ingots. The company also manufactures tons of fertilizer each year.

Surface building, Sullivan mine, Kimberley, British Columbia, 1930
— *Courtesy Provincial Archives, Victoria, British Columbia.*

Like mining, Kootenai Valley agriculture has continued to support many families. On the American side of the border, a recession in farm prices in the 1920s followed by the Great Depression reduced the value of agricultural production in the valley. World War II brought a farming boom, and after the war, production remained high. The main agricultural centers in Lincoln County are the Tobacco Plains and the southern Kootenai Valley. Products include livestock, hay, vegetables, apples, and strawberries. The valley in northern Idaho has more valuable farmland than the Montana section. From Bonners Ferry to the Canadian border, reclaimed bottomlands have produced excellent yields of wheat and oats. Hay and other forage crops have grown well on benchlands above the valley's floor.

In Canada, ranches and farms cover much of the Kootenai Valley and the land around Kootenay Lake. The lake region was the scene of an early Twentieth Century boom in fruit orchards. Promoters of the area flooded England with pamphlets, and many British gentlemen troubled by high costs at home found a new life of leisure raising fruit in west Kootenai. They turned wilderness into orchards and built large, vine-covered houses with fireplaces and elaborate gardens. Fruit ranching reached a peak in 1922 when railroad cars and boats hauled many loads of fruit from the region. Eventually the several local fruit raisers' unions amalgamated to form the Associated Growers. By the thirties, prices had declined, and cherry blight had wiped out many orchards. One by one, ranchers quit growing fruit. Many sold their land for housing developments. Unfortunately, the Kootenay Lake fruit boom died as quickly as it had been born.

Near Creston, where the Kootenai River flows into the lake, the thirties brought the beginnings of a vast reclamation project. Eventually, fifty-three dikes blocked off the waters of the Kootenai and put more than twenty-five thousand acres of rich bottomland into production. Serious floods in 1938 and 1948 forced the industrious farmers to rebuild their dikes. Today this land grows large crops of hay, cereal grains, potatoes, strawberries, and peas. Baillie-Grohman's dream has been realized.

Among the most unique farmers of the lower Kootenai area

Sullivan mine in 1945 — *Courtesy Provincial Archives, Victoria, British Columbia.*

Orchards near Creston, British Columbia — *Courtesy Provincial Archives, Victoria, British Columbia.*

Harvest display in Libby, Montana, 1911 — *Courtesy Lincoln County Library, Libby, Montana.*

have been the Doukhobors. Members of this religious sect came to Canada from Russia to escape the persecution of the Czarist regime. Their simple religious ideology stated that every man must follow the spirit of God throughout his life. They resisted state leadership by refusing to bear arms, fill out census forms, or pay taxes. The immigrants originally settled in Saskatchewan, but beginning in 1908, many moved to the lower Kootenai near Castlegar and Brilliant.

The Kootenai Doukhobor communities consisted of brick buildings housing from thirty to fifty people each. The people worked long and hard, clearing land, planting orchards, and constructing a sawmill and jam factory. The history of the Kootenai Doukhobors has been filled with strife and violence. Frequent clashes with the government have resulted from the sect's resistance to state authority. Violent outbursts, such as dynamiting and burning of buildings, have often been blamed on a radical Doukhobor faction, the Sons of Freedom. Today, most Doukhobors have been integrated into society's mainstream, and their socialistic life style is gradually disappearing.

Wing Dam, Upper Bonnington Falls, British Columbia — *Courtesy Provincial Archives, Victoria, British Columbia.*

During the Second World War, the Kootenai region harbored another major ethnic community, the Japanese Canadians. These people migrated from the coast to the interior, not by choice, but because of the policy of forced relocation imposed by the Canadian government. Many of the fifteen thousand resettled Japanese were sent to the Slocan ghost towns of Sandon, New Denver, and Kaslo. Here they reconditioned old buildings, constructed schools and hospitals, and engaged in logging and agriculture. They were never happy in their uprooted circumstances, and most of them either returned to their old homes or went back to Japan following the war.

Those few Japanese who chose to stay have witnessed the development of numerous new industries in Canada's Kootenai Valley. In the early 1960s, a large brewery began operations at Creston. To the east at Cranbrook, many new plants have appeared within the last ten years, including an engine-rebuilding plant and a cement factory. An industrial park, opened in 1969, houses more than thirty companies. All this has made Cranbrook the fastest growing city in the entire Kootenai Valley.

Harvesting Christmas trees, Lincoln County, Montana — *Courtesy* The Western News, *Libby, Montana.*

In Montana's Lincoln County, the Christmas tree industry which began in 1916 has grown steadily. Today Eureka is known as the "Christmas Tree Capital of the World." Beginning in October each year, hundreds find employment as cutters, bailers, taggers, inspectors, loaders, and truckers, preparing the several hundred carloads of trees which the area's forests provide annually. In 1958, this industry received national recognition when the White House Christmas tree, a seventy-four-foot Engleman spruce, came from the Kootenai National Forest.

With industrial and population growth in the Kootenai Valley, there has been a concomitant increased need for electrical energy. This has necessitated the tapping of a source of wealth on the Kootenai River undreamed of by the early-day Indians, trappers, and miners.

In 1896, the need for cheap electricity in mining and smelting operations led to the incorporation of Canada's West Kootenay Power and Light Company. This firm built a dam and hydroelectric plant at Lower Bonnington Falls on the Kootenai River between Kootenay Lake and the river's junction with the Colum-

133

Working on Upper Bonnington Falls Dam, 1906 — *Courtesy Provincial Archives, Victoria, British Columbia.*

bia. The company constructed four additional power dams on this fast-flowing section of the river during the next half-century. By the early 1940s, the harnessed energy of the Kootenai had made West Kootenay Power and Light the largest producer of electricity in all of British Columbia. These five power plants, spaced at four-mile intervals, produce well over 200,000 horsepower. Much of this energy has gone into generating Trail's smelters. The company later erected cables to send power from the dams to the Sullivan Mine at Kimberley. The section of this cable spanning Kootenay Lake was, at the time of its construction, the world's longest unsupported cable at just under two miles.

Until recent years, no one attempted to harness the waters of the American Kootenai River for electricity. The power for the towns along the river came from small local power plants or outside sources. Some rural areas, such as the Yaak Valley, had no electricity at all until the 1960s. Several groups made plans to construct power dams on the river, and in 1914, the Kootenai Power Construction Company even received government permission to build a dam at Kootenai Falls west of Libby. But such schemes all ended in failure. Not until the conclusion of the American Canadian International Agreement in the mid-1960s did construction begin on the huge dam east of Libby, which not only would harness the energy of the river but also would prevent the costly floods which had plagued Kootenai Valley settlers since the days of the first pioneers.

9

Libby Dam

The story of the first dam on the American Kootenai is a narrative of the persistence of many individuals in two nations. Their determined efforts overcame both the international complications which long delayed initiation of the project and the physical problems posed by the construction itself. The more than thirty years which passed between conception and completion of Libby Dam is indicative of the magnitude of the obstacles which had to be surmounted.

In September of 1943, the United States Senate passed a resolution proposing a review of the Columbia River and its tributaries to determine the area's hydroelectric and flood-control needs. In that same year, the U.S. Army revised its "Plan 308" which it had issued in 1932. Revised "Plan 308" called for the authorization of three dams on the Columbia River, one on Idaho's Snake River, and a 239 million dollar dam on the Kootenai River near Libby.

During the next five years, the Army held numerous public hearings throughout the region of the proposed projects. During two of these meetings in Libby, Colonel L. H. Hewitt of the Army Corps of Engineers emphasized that the primary purpose of the dam at Libby would be flood control. People from Bonners Ferry, Idaho, and Creston, British Columbia, attended the second Libby meeting in July of 1948 and urged immediate action on the plan. During the preceding spring, they had witnessed the worst flooding in fifty years along the entire course of the Kootenai.

Libby Dam site, October 1968 — *Courtesy U.S. Corps of Engineers.*

Early in 1950, the Eighty-first Congress debated a large flood-control bill which included authorization for the construction of Libby Dam. In April, the Senate passed the bill by a comfortable majority. The following month, the bill, pushed strongly by Montana's western district Congressman Mike Mansfield, received House approval and President Truman's signature. The act contained no appropriated funds but authorized Congress to spend fifty-three million dollars for Libby Dam. Colonel E. C. Itschner, Seattle District Engineer, speculated that construction on the dam could begin as early as July 1951.

The proposed dam would back up water forty-two miles into Canada. The project therefore required the approval of the six-man American-Canadian International Joint Commission created by a 1909 boundary waters treaty. In March 1951, the International Joint Commission held public hearings in cities on both sides of the border. At these meetings, upper valley farmers and officials of Canada's East Kootenay River and Light Company requested compensation for the damage the lake would cause. Most of those present, especially residents of the lower valley, favored the project.

Top view of Libby Dam construction trestle — *Courtesy U.S. Corps of Engineers*

Compensation for flooded Canadian land proved to be the issue which led to a stalemate between the Canadian and the American members of the International Joint Commission. The Canadians, led by Commission co-chairman A.G.L. McNaughton, demanded up to thirty percent of the power generated at the proposed dam in repayment for Canada's land which would be flooded. The American representatives advocated a one-time cash settlement for all of the Canadian damage claims.

Despite this impasse, planning on the dam continued in earnest, supported by funds authorized by Congress. Early in 1952, the Corps of Engineers awarded a contract for foundation exploration. Workers began to drill test tunnels to determine the best location for the dam. Others studied possible routes for the Great Northern Railway tracks which would need to be relocated once the lake waters began to rise.

But by 1953, Congress had cut off funds for project planning because of the continued inability of the International Joint Commission to reach an agreement. Officials such as Montana's Governor John Bonner urged the Americans on the Commission

Holing out Flathead Tunnel — *Courtesy U.S. Corps of Engineers.*

to stand firm. In a letter to co-chairman A. O. Stanley, Governor Bonner wrote, "I believe that such a grant of power to Canada would be against the best interests of the state of Montana and the United States." McNaughton, in turn, told the House of Commons External Affairs Committee: "They [the Americans] must compensate us in terms of the only unit in which we are prepared to deal, and that is in terms of power."

All resistance to the proposed dam did not come from Canada. The Libby Chamber of Commerce and officials of Libby's two major industries, the J. Neils Lumber Company and the Zonolite Company, voiced strong opposition to a project site two miles northeast of Libby which the Corps of Engineers had been considering. They argued that a dam there would flood both the Zonolite mines and much of the timberland which supported the Neils Company. They did not oppose the dam itself but called for location of the project farther downstream.

In April 1953, Secretary of State John Foster Dulles, acting on a request by the Chief of the Army Engineers, withdrew the American application for approval of Libby Dam from the Inter-

Interior view of the Burlington Northern Flathead tunnel — *Courtesy U.S. Corps of Engineers.*

national Joint Commission. Dulles noted that the United States wished to re-examine "certain domestic questions," such as a selection of the location for the dam. Other official reasons given for the decision included the new Eisenhower administration's desire for economy and a proposal to build the dam below Libby, putting the reservoir all within American territory. At the same time, several U.S. Senators moved to secure Congressional cancellation of Libby Dam.

Despite this strong opposition, Montana Senator James E. Murray secured a further appropriation of funds for continued project planning. By the end of 1953, Army Engineers and Libby citizens had agreed that a dam site seventeen miles above Libby appeared physically and economically suitable. The following April, the United States again placed the proposed dam before the International Joint Commission, and in September, President Eisenhower spoke out in favor of the project.

Once again, however, the proposal hit an impasse, as the Canadian Government continued to demand one-third of the power from the dam. This led both the Americans and Canadians on the Commission to consider alternate power and flood-control projects in the Columbia region. By early 1955, McNaughton informed the Americans that serious discussion of Libby Dam could not take place for at least fifteen months while Canadian engineers studied water storage and diversion possibilities within Canada. Among the plans the Canadians were considering was a resurrection of Baillie-Grohman's scheme to divert the Kootenai into the headwaters of the Columbia at Canal Flats. Meanwhile, Libby Dam plans remained at a virtual standstill despite repeated prodding of the International Joint Commission by Montana Senator Mike Mansfield.

For the next three years, the Commission did next to nothing on the Libby Dam question. In 1956, Montana Congressman Lee Metcalf, with Mansfield's support, urged Congress to appropriate funds to build a "two-story" dam. The first section would back water only to the international border, so it could be built at once without Canadian approval. The Army Engineers opposed Metcalf's plan as economically impractical, and no further action was taken.

Libby Dam site, January 1971 — *Courtesy U.S. Corps of Engineers.*

Libby Dam site after the January 1971 rock slide — *Courtesy U.S. Corps of Engineers.*

Late in 1957, the Corps of Engineers again held public hearings to review the entire Columbia Basin water-development plan. The following summer, members of the International Joint Commission visited dams and prospective dam sites throughout the Pacific Northwest, including Libby. This tour helped bring about an understanding between American and Canadian members of the Commission regarding the power and flood-control needs of each nation. By the end of the year, both McNaughton and acting Canadian Prime Minister Howard Green were expressing optimism that the American-Canadian deadlock over Columbia Basin development would soon be broken.

Still, progress toward an understanding proceeded slowly. In April of 1959, the United States finally agreed to reimburse Canada for storing water on Canadian sites which, on release, would develop power at American dams. Not until December did the International Joint Commission produce a general plan for cooperative development of the Columbia Basin suitable to both countries.

Differences persisted over the specific issue of Libby Dam. The Canadians wished to build dams near the Arrow Lakes and on Mica Creek before beginning construction at Libby, but the Americans urged immediate building of the dam on the loop of the Kootenai. Meanwhile, Mansfield and Metcalf continued to call for construction of the dam in two stages. Mansfield even suggested that the dam be built on the American-Canadian boundary as a symbol of international cooperation.

Finally, in October of 1960, President Eisenhower and Canada's Prime Minister Diefenbaker announced that negotiators, after months of talks, had reached an agreement on provisions for a Columbia Basin joint development treaty. Included in the document was Canadian authorization to let forty-two miles of Canada's Kootenai valley be flooded by a dam near Libby. In a ceremony at the White House on January 17, 1961, Eisenhower and Diefenbaker signed the treaty for cooperative development of the Columbia basin, which contained the statement:

The United States of America for a period of five years from the ratification date, has the option to commence construction of a dam on the Kootenai River near Libby, Montana, to provide storage to meet flood control and other purposes in the United States of America.

The treaty called for Canada to begin construction of three dams as soon as possible on Mica Creek, near the Arrow Lakes, and near Duncan Lake. By controlling the annual flow of the Columbia, these three dams would enable American dams downstream to produce vast amounts of additional power. Another clause entitled Canada to one-half of the power benefits gained by American facilities on the lower Columbia as a result of the regulating effect of the Canadian dams. The document entitled the United States to all power produced at Libby Dam.

In March, when the Senate considered the treaty, no one spoke out in opposition. Montana Senator Lee Metcalf called it "an accomplishment of internal comity and international friendship." Idaho's Frank Church added that in taming the Kootenai, Libby Dam would "demonstrate again that man is not powerless to control his environment." The Senate passed the treaty by a ninety-to-one vote. Congress then appropriated funds to continue planning on the dam, and the Corps of Engineers returned to the Libby area to resume exploratory work.

Buttress to prevent slides near Libby Dam — *Courtesy U.S. Corps of Engineers.*

In Canada, the ratification process did not proceed so smoothly. Canadian law required both the federal government and the British Columbia provincial government to approve the treaty. The provincial government became involved in a plan to sell power produced on the Peace River in British Columbia. Government officials feared that the addition of Libby Dam to the northwest power pool would ruin this scheme, and so they refused to ratify the Columbia Treaty. Furthermore, British Columbia would not act on the treaty until the exact price and amount of power benefits to be delivered from the United States had been determined. Provincial officials hoped to sell this power to American buyers in order to finance the three treaty dams to be built in Canada.

Despite this stalemate, the Corps of Engineers continued survey work throughout 1962 and 1963. They placed the tentative damsite seventeen miles upstream from Libby. The deadlock over the treaty caused repeated postponement of the starting date for construction.

In May 1963, American President Kennedy and Canadian Prime Minister Pearson moved to break the stalemate. They arranged a protocol which the two governments signed the following January. This agreement called for a United States purchaser to buy Canada's half of the treaty power generated in the United States over the next thirty years for a lump sum of 245 million dollars. British Columbia would then use this money to finance construction of the storage dams at Mica Creek, Arrow Lakes, and Duncan Lake. After another delay of six months, the Canadian and British Columbian governments signed the treaty.

On September 16, 1964, President Johnson and Prime Minister Pearson met at the International Peace Arch on the American-Canadian boundary near Blaine, Washington, and participated in the ceremony which inaugurated development of the Columbia River Basin. After two decades of false hopes and frustrating delays, the two nations had cleared the way to begin construction of Libby Dam.

Throughout 1964, designers worked on final project plans. They called for a concrete gravity structure 3,055 feet long, rising 420 feet above bedrock. The dam would require enough concrete to build a two-lane highway from New York to Salt Lake City, Utah. Upon completion it would store more than 5.8 million acre-feet of water and back up a lake forty-two miles across the Canadian border. The U.S. Army Corps of Engineers and the

Montana's longest auto bridge spanning Lake Koocanusa — *Courtesy U.S. Corps of Engineers.*

U.S. Forest Service planned numerous recreation areas along the lake for the millions of anticipated visitors. The dam was designed to house eight generators which would produce a total of 840 thousand kilowatts of power to be marketed and distributed by the Bonneville Power Administration, an agency of the Department of the Interior. Even more costly than construction of the dam itself would be the relocation of 118 miles of roads and highways and sixty miles of Great Northern Railway tracks, involving a seven-mile tunnel through Elk Mountain. Lake inundation and railway relocation also called for the acquisition of more than thirty-eight thousand acres of government and private land.

In January of 1965, the American government officially informed the Canadians that it would build Libby Dam under the terms of the 1961 treaty. Army engineers scheduled construction to begin in 1966. In the spring of that year, the Corps began awarding contracts for the railroad relocation project, and work commenced on the Great Northern tunnel near the town of Trego, Montana. By that time, the architectural designs for the

Relocated town site, Rexford, Montana — *Courtesy U.S. Corps of Engineers.*

dam had been completed. Formulated with the assistance of a private consulting architect, plans called for an integration of the dam with its natural environment. This marked the first time aesthetic values were seriously considered on such a project. A visitors center, located on the right abutment, would serve as the resident engineer's office during the construction period. A treaty tower was planned for the top of the dam structure to give visitors an unobstructed view of the lake and to stand as a monument of international cooperation.

American-Canadian unity was much in evidence during the August 13, 1966, ceremonies which officially began construction of Libby Dam. As part of Operation BOLD (Blast Off Libby Dam), Senator Mike Mansfield, who had labored tirelessly to secure approval of the project, set off a dynamite blast to inaugurate the operation. Mansfield told the audience of two thousand visitors from both sides of the border: "The turning of the earth here today signals the beginning of a new prosperity for northwestern Montana."

The following spring, the Corps of Engineers awarded the

contract for building the dam to a combine headed by Morrison-Knudsen Company of Boise, Idaho. Work began at once on the dam's west abutment. Unlike many similar projects, Libby Dam did not involve diverting the river through a tunnel. Instead, workers built a low cofferdam which, by early 1968, channeled the waters of the Kootenai along the west side of the valley. Work then began on the east half of the dam.

For building the dam itself, a huge 275-foot-high steel trestle eventually spanned the canyon. Two parallel tracks stretched across the deck of the trestle, enabling trains to deliver materials to placement sites. Huge whirley cranes lowered the buckets which placed concrete into the dam's monoliths at a rate of 4,200 cubic yards per day. Initially, crews erected only the left half of the trestle for work on the first section of the dam.

On June 1, 1968, a public "bucket busting" ceremony involving dignitaries from both sides of the border marked the first pouring of the dam's 3.7 million cubic yards of concrete. By the end of the year, workers had completed the first stage of concrete placement on the left abutment. They then built a second-stage cofferdam which diverted the Kootenai between two completed blocks on the left side of the dam. This enabled the trestle to be completed so that work could begin on the right side.

Meanwhile, eight separate contractors continued the work of railway relocation. On June 21, 1968, President Johnson pressed a button in the White House, setting off the blast which holed through the seven-mile Flathead Tunnel. Crews then placed concrete and ventilation equipment in the Western Hemisphere's second longest railway tunnel. Work also began on relocation of the highways which eventually would span both sides of the reservoir.

A project of such immensity as Libby Dam naturally created social and economic problems in sparsely populated Lincoln County. Valley landholders severely criticized the federal government for acquiring land outside the flooded area to be used for recreation sites. The Montana Fish and Game Department urged the Corps of Engineers to pay a social cost for the reservoir's destruction of fish and wildlife. Army engineers finally agreed to build a fish hatchery for the state of Montana.

The dam also had a great impact on the government of Lincoln County. The influx of more than two thousand construction workers placed heavy demands on services such as education, law enforcement, licensing, traffic control, assessments, welfare,

President Gerald Ford at Libby Dam dedication ceremonies —
Courtesy U.S. Corps of Engineers.

Completed Libby Dam — *Courtesy U.S. Corps of Engineers.*

and sanitation. Shortage of space and qualified teachers plagued the schools of the county. Here the Corps of Engineers helped to solve the problem. In Libby, the Corps built thirty-six classrooms and paid one-third of the cost of a new junior high school. In Eureka, they built ten new classrooms and helped to finance a new elementary school. Army engineers also constructed rural classrooms throughout eastern Lincoln County. In addition, the Corps helped to construct a new airfield at Libby and erected a new forest ranger station at Canoe Gulch.

The citizens of the town of Rexford, Montana, experienced the greatest of all changes wrought by the Libby project. The Corps of Engineers relocated the entire town on land above the old townsite which eventually was inundated by the reservoir. They constructed a new school, post office, town hall, fire station, and new water, power, and sewage facilities.

As work progressed on the project, Canadians fulfilled their share of the Columbia Treaty bargain. In 1967, they completed the 2,600-foot-wide, earth-filled dam across the Duncan River north of Kootenay Lake. Two years later, they dedicated Arrow

Dam on the Columbia near Castlegar. The concrete dam had to be equipped with a navigation lock for river traffic. The largest of the three Canadian treaty dams, the Mica Dam on the Columbia north of Revelstoke, was finished in 1973. This structure rises over eight hundred feet from the valley floor and backs up the waters of the Columbia for one hundred and forty-five miles.

By the end of 1969, construction at Libby was on schedule and fifty-five percent complete despite Nixon administration budget cuts which reduced funds for the 1970 fiscal year by four million dollars. Late 1970 marked the completion of Montana's longest highway bridge. The 2,347-foot structure spanned the future reservoir thirty-two miles upstream from the dam. In November, a special train made the first official run along the newly completed Burlington Northern Railway line. The following month, the House of Representatives approved the acronym Lake Koocanusa as the official name for the new reservoir.

On January 31, 1971, nature disrupted progress on Libby Dam when tons of rock crashed down the mountainside near the east abutment. Fortunately, the slide occurred when no one was working. If it had happened during the construction season, the area of the disaster would have been alive with activity. The slide destroyed the contractor's main power substation and severely damaged the concrete refrigeration plant. The Libby Dam Board of Consultants, which had been involved in solving problems of the project from its beginning, held a series of meetings to discuss the slide. Upon its recommendation, Army engineers studied the stability of the ridges on the left bank and constructed a rock fill buttress at the base of the ridges to provide greater stability.

The slide delayed concrete placement for only a few months. By August 1971, workers had diverted the river through temporary sluice gates and had closed the final block of the dam. The water in Lake Koocanusa then began to rise. Although fund limitations placed the over-all project slightly behind schedule in 1971 and 1972, dam construction remained on time.

In April, 1972, the Corps of Engineers gave out the final big contract — one for construction of the powerhouse. Separate firms began work on the turbines and generators. In March, 1973, the Kootenai began flowing through the dam's permanent sluices, and four months later, crews placed the final bucket of concrete.

The last year of dam construction involved removal of the

trestle and cranes, finishing the interior of dam facilities, continuing work on the powerhouse, and landscaping in the area of the dam and along the lake. Army engineers and biologists also labored to solve the problem of nitrogen saturation in the water flowing through the permanent sluices. This was killing thousands of fish in the river below the dam, according to Montana Fish and Game Department biologists. In October of 1976, after frustrating delays, the Corps announced that planning would begin on the long-promised fish hatchery. Construction began in May, 1978 on this two million dollar structure, designed to produce about fifty thousand pounds of trout each year. Nitrogen saturation below the dam also diminished markedly once water began flowing through the powerhouse rather than over the spillway.

In July 1973, building of Libby Dam was finished in time to meet the seven-year construction period allotted by the International Treaty. This completion did not mark the end of problems. In Lincoln County, local officials and other citizens expressed discontent with the project. Complaints centered on the reservoir's destruction of wildlife habitat and what some called the "boom-bust" cycle created by the dam, with an accompanying decline in the local tax base. Budget problems led to delays in construction of promised recreation facilities on the lake.

Corps of Engineer officials endeavored to meet the criticism. Army Engineers took over responsibility for building recreation facilities after budget cutbacks prevented the U.S. Forest Service from handling them. Project Manager Bob Sato pointed out that the Corps was working to "maintain a superior visitation program at the dam" to offset the loss of local tax base caused by flooding of formerly private lands. The Corps also helped the Montana Fish and Game Department and the U.S. Forest Service to acquire additional tracts of wildlife range to mitigate that lost to the reservoir.

In 1975, officials prepared for the dedication of Libby Dam amid an atmosphere of growing concern over environmental preservation and a world-wide energy shortage. American-Canadian disagreement, which had delayed the project's commencement for so long, was again in evidence during the August 24 ceremonies. Several Canadian officials, including Prime Minister Pierre Trudeau, declined to attend. Leaders of British Columbia's provincial government expressed concern over Lake Koocanusa's flooding of Canadian wildlife habitat. Premier

Libby Dam and Lake Koocanusa — *Courtesy U.S. Corps of Engineers.*

David Barrett had voiced discontent over the power sale provisions of the 1963 treaty. His government threatened to resurrect the idea of diverting Kootenai River water across Canal Flats into the Columbia in order to generate additional power in the new dams north of the border. Finally, the Canadians were threatening to cut off further exportation of oil and natural gas into Montana.

Despite all of the problems, both American President Gerald Ford and Canadian Minister of Energy Donald MacDonald expressed hope during the dedication that their respective nations would be able to cooperate in solving future crises. Ford lauded the multipurpose benefits which would be derived from Libby Dam. The two then switched on the first of the eight huge hydroelectric units which ultimately would produce 840 kilowatts of badly needed electricity from the facility.

Thus the wealth of the Kootenai will continue to be relied upon by both the basin residents and people hundreds of miles distant, many of whom have never heard of the river whose harnessed power is lighting their homes. As man's supply of energy continues to become more and more limited, the hydroelectricity produced by the river as it tumbles down the western slopes of the Rockies may well prove to be far more precious than the furs, minerals, timber, and farm products which have come from the land of the Kootenai.

Sources

Books

Angus, H. F., Howay, F.W., and Sage, W.N. *British Columbia and the United States*. Toronto: The Ryerson Press, 1942.

Atwood, Wallace W. *The Rocky Mountains*. New York: The Vanguard Press, 1945.

Baillie-Grohman, W. A. *Fifteen Years' Sport and Life in the Hunting Grounds of Western America and British Columbia*. London: Horace Cox, 1900.

Baker, Paul E. *The Forgotten Kootenai*. Boise: Mountain States Press, Inc., 1955.

Bancroft, Hubert H. *History of British Columbia 1792-1887*. San Francisco: The History Company Publishers, 1887.

Barlee, N. L. *Gold Creeks and Ghost Towns*. Summerland, B.C.: Canada West Magazine, Undated.

Berton, Pierre. *The Impossible Railway: The Building of the Canadian Pacific*. New York: Alfred A. Knopf, 1972.

Brad, Jacoba Boothman. *Homestead on the Kootenai*. Caldwell, Idaho: Caxton Printers Ltd., 1960.

Defebaugh, James E. *History of the Lumber Industry of America*. Vol. I. Chicago: The American Lumberman, 1906.

DeSmet, Pierre Jean. *Oregon Mission and Travels over the Rocky Mountains, 1845-48*. Reprinted in Thwaites, Reuben G., (ed.). *Early Western Travels, 1748-1846* XXIX. Cleveland: The Arthur H. Clark Company, 1906.

Federal Writers Project of the Works Progress Administration. *The Idaho Encyclopedia*. Caldwell, Idaho: Caxton Printers Ltd., 1938.

Glover, Richard (ed.). *David Thompson's Narrative 1784-1812.* Toronto: The Champlain Society, 1962.

Gould, Ed. *Logging: British Columbia's Logging History.* Saanichton, B.C.: Hancod House Publishers Ltd., 1975.

Graham, Clara. *Fur and Gold in the Kootenays.* Vancouver, B.C.: Wrigley Printing Co. Ltd., 1945.

———. *Kootenay Mosaic.* Vancouver, B.C.: Evergreen Press Ltd., 1963.

———. *This Was the Kootenay.* Vancouver, B.C.: Evergreen Press Ltd., 1973.

Holbrook, Stewart. *The Columbia.* New York: Rinehart and Co., Inc., 1956.

Howe, R. S. (ed.). *The Great Northern Country.* New York: Great Northern Railway and Northern Steamship Co., Undated.

Johnson, Olga W. *Early Libby and Troy Montana.* Libby, Montana: Olga W. Johnson, 1958.

———. *Flathead and Kootenai.* Glendale, California: Arthur H. Clark Co., 1969.

Kay, David, and D. A. MacDonald. *Come with Me to Yesterday: Tales Retold of Pioneer Days in East Kootenay.* Cranbrook, B.C.: Rocky Mountain Printing, 1972.

Libby Pioneer Society and Libby Womens Club. *Nuggets to Timber: Pioneer Days at Libby, Montana.* Libby, Montana: The Western News, 1970.

Magaret, Helene. *Father DeSmet, Pioneer Priest of the Rockies.* New York: Farrar & Rinehart, Inc., 1940.

McDougall, J. Lorne. *Canadian Pacific.* Montreal: McGill University Press, 1968.

Mills, Randall. *Stern Wheelers up Columbia.* Palo Alto, California: Pacific Books, 1947.

Neils, Paul. *Julius Neils and the J. Neils Lumber Company.* Seattle: Frank McCaffrey Publishers, 1971.

Norris, John. *Strangers Entertained: A History of the Ethnic Groups of British Columbia.* Vancouver, B.C.: Evergreen Press Ltd., 1971.

Ormsby, Margaret A. *British Columbia: A History.* Vancouver, B.C.: The MacMillan Company of Canada Ltd., 1958.

Pioneers of Tobacco Plains Country. *The Story of the Tobacco Plains Country.* Caldwell, Idaho: Caxton Printers, Ltd., 1950.

Rodney, William. *Kootenai Brown, His Life and Times, 1839-1916.* Sidney, B.C.: Gray's Publishing Ltd., 1969.

Ronan, Peter. *History of the Flathead Indians.* Minneapolis: Ross & Haines Inc., 1890.

Schraff, Robert. *Canada's Mountain National Parks.* New York: David McKay Company, Inc., 1966.

Schuchert, Charles, and Dunbar, Carl O. *A Textbook of Geology: Part II, Historical Geology.* New York: John Wiley & Sons, Inc., 1941.

Scott, David, and Hanic, Edna H. *Nelson: Queen City of the Kootenays.* Vancouver, B.C.: Mitchell Press Ltd., 1972.

Smyth, Fred J. *Tales of the Kootenays.* Cranbrook, B.C.: Office of The Courier, 1942.

Spencer, Betty Goodwin. *The Big Blowup.* Caldwell, Idaho: Caxton Printers Ltd., 1956.

Spry, Irene M. (ed.). *The Papers of the Palliser Expedition 1857-1860.* Toronto: The Champlain Society, 1968.

Tyrell, J. B. (ed.). *David Thompson's Narrative on His Explorations in Western America 1784-1812.* Toronto: The Champlain Society, 1916.

White, M. Catherine (ed.). *David Thompson's Journals Relating To Montana and Adjacent Regions, 1808-1812.* Missoula, Montana: Montana State University Press, 1950.

Williams, Glyndwr (ed.). *London Correspondence Inward from Sir George Simpson 1841-42.* London: The Hudson's Bay Record Society, 1973.

Journal Articles

Antrei, Albert. "Father Pierce Jean DeSmet." *Montana, The Magazine of Western History*, XIII (April, 1963), 24-43.

Doak, William E. "Pioneer Steamboating on the Kootenai River in Montana." *The Montana Magazine of History*, II (April, 1952), 49-55.

Ewers, John C. "Iroquois Indians in the Far West." *Montana, The Magazine of Western History*, XIII (April, 1963), 2-10.

Fitzsimmons, James. "Columbia River Chronicles." *British Columbia Historical Quarterly*, I (April, 1937), 87-100.

Fletcher, Marvin. "Army Fire Fighters." *Idaho Yesterdays*, XVI (January, 1952), 1-52.

Hidy, Ralph. "Lumbermen in Idaho." *Idaho Yesterdays*, VI (Winter, 1962), 2-17.

Johnson, Olga W. "Thriving in the Loop of the Kootenai: Libby and Troy." *Montana, The Magazine of Western History*, XVI (July, 1966), 44-55.

Jordan, Mabel E. "The Kootenay Reclamation and Colonization Scheme and William Adolph Baillie-Grohman." *British Columbia Historical Quarterly*, XX (July, 1956), 187-220.

Josephy, Alvin M., Jr. "The Naming of the Nez Perce." *Montana, The Magazine of Western History*, V (October, 1955), 4-18.

Malouf, Carling, "Early Kutenai History." *The Montana Magazine of History*, II (April, 1952), 5-9.

Turnbull, Elsie. "Old Mines on the West Koonenay." *British Columbia Historical Quarterly*, XX (July, 1956), 147-163.

Wells, Merle W. "A House for Trading." *Idaho Yesterdays*, III (Fall, 1959), 22-26.

Newspapers and Magazines

The Courier (Cranbrook, B.C.)

The Greats Fall Tribune

The Kootenai Times (Libby, Montana)

The Missoulian (Missoula, Montana)

Montana Rural Electric News

Tobacco Valley News (Eureka, Montana)

The Western News (Libby, Montana)

Other Published Sources

The British Columbia Forest Industries 1967 Yearbook. Vancouver, B.C.: Journal of Commerce Ltd., 1967.

Camsell, Charles. *Geology of the Canadian National Parks.* Ottawa: Department of the Interior, 1914.

Chamberlain, Alexander F. "The Kootenay Indians." *Annual Archeological Report No. 12.* Toronto, 1905, 178-187.

Construction Progress Report, Libby Dam Project (10 reports). U.S. Army Corps of Engineers, Seattle District.

Daly, Reginald A. *Geology of the North American Cordillera at the Forty-Ninth Parallel.* Ottawa: Canada Department of Mines Geological Survey No. 38, 1912.

Dyson, James L. *The Geologic Story of Glacier National Park.* Special Bulletin No. 3, Glacier Natural History Association, 1953.

Johns, Willis M. *Progress Report on Geologic Investigations in the Kootenai-Flathead Area, Northwest Montana: No. 1, Western Lincoln County.* Butte: Montana Bureau of Mines and Geology Bulletin No. 12, 1959.

Perry, Eugene. *Montana in the Geologic Past.* Butte: Montana Bureau of Mines and Geology Bulletin No. 26, 1962.

The Province of British Columbia Centennial Directory. Vancouver, B.C.: Centenary Committee, 1967.

Schofield, Stuart J. *Geology of Cranbrook Map-Area, British Columbia.* Ottawa: Canada Department of Mines Geological Survey Memoir No. 76, 1915.

Taylor, Dee C. *Archeological Investigations in the Libby Reservoir Area, Northwestern Montana.* Missoula, Montana: University of Montana Contributions to Anthropology No. 3, 1973.

Turney-High, Harry Holbert. *Ethnography of the Kutenai.* Memoirs of the American Anthropological Association, No. 56, 1941.

U.S. Congress, Senate. 87th Congress, 1st Session. March 16, 1961. *Congressional Record* CVII, 4131-4144.

U.S. Forest Service. Agriculture Information Bulletin No. 83. *Highlights in the History of Forest Conservation.* 1968.

Work Projects Administration Inventory of the County Archives of Montana. Bozeman: Historical Records Survey, 1940.

Unpublished Sources

Cottingham, Mollie E. "A History of the West Kootenay District in British Columbia." Unpublished Master's thesis, Vancouver: University of British Columbia, 1947.

Griffing, John M. "An Analysis of the Libby Dam Construction Impact on Local Government Operations." Unpublished Master's thesis, Missoula: University of Montana, 1968.

Isch, Flora Mae Bellefleur. "The Development of the Upper Flathead and Kootenai Country." Unpublished Master's thesis, Missoula: Montana State University, 1948.

Malouf, Carling. "Economy and Land Use by the Indians of Western Montana, U.S.A." Unpublished Manuscript, Missoula: Montana State University, 1952.

Montana Federation of Womens Clubs. "Local Community History of Libby, Montana." Unpublished Manuscript, Libby, Montana, 1926.

Morrow, Delores. "Our Sawdust Roots: A History of the Forest Products Industry in Montana." Unpublished Manuscript, Missoula: University of Montana, 1973.

Thrupp, Sylvia L. "A History of the Cranbrook District in East Kootenay." Unpublished Master's thesis, Vancouver: University of British Columbia, 1929.

Chambers of Commerce That Sent Information to the Author

Bonners Ferry, Idaho

Cranbrook, British Columbia

Creston, British Columbia

Kimberley, British Columbia

Kootenay National Park, British Columbia

Nelson, British Columbia

Index

Abbott, John, 72
Abraham, Kutenai Chief, 44, 49
Agriculture, 72-75, 128, 129
Ainsworth, George, 57
Airplanes, 118, 119
Allen, Steven, 49
Alley, E. N., 126
Annerly, *82*, 86
Armstrong, Francis Patrick, 84, 86, 88, 91
Arrow Dam, 150
Arrow Lakes, 6, 60, 143
Associated Growers, 129
Astorian Company, 30, 31, 32
Athabaska Pass, 30-33

Baillie-Grohman, William A., 75-78, 91, 103, 129, 141
Baird-Harper Sawmill, *109*
Baker, Colonel James, 74, 98
Banff-Windermere Road, *121*, 123, 124
Banner and Bangle Mine, 68, 72
Barrett, David, 153
Berland, Edward, 33
Big Ledge, 55, 57
Birch, Arthur N., 46
Bitterroot Valley, 35
Blackfeet Indians, 8, 14, 24, 30, 35, 37, 43
Blaine, Washington, 145
Blakiston, Thomas, 41, 42
Blanchet, Fr., 35
Blue Bell Mine, *54*, 57

Bonner, Edwin L., 51
Bonner, John, 138
Bonners Ferry, Idaho, 7, 12, 28, 50, 84, 92, *101*, 124, 128, 136; first settlement, 51; founded, 93, 95; railroads, 96, 99, 102; sawmills, 109, 111, *115*, 117
Bonners Ferry Lumber Company, 109-111, *115*, 117
Bonneville Power Administration, 146
Bonnington Falls, *132-134*
Boulder Creek, 126
Bourgeau, Eugene, 41-43
Bourgeois, Joe, 65
Breckenridge, John, 104
Brilliant, British Columbia, 131
Brydges and Fisher Sawmill, *112*
Burchette, Walter, 66

Cabinet Mountains, 1
Canadian Pacific Railway, 63, 76, 79-81, 84, 89, 92, 94-96, 99, 102
Canal Flats, 77, 84, 86, 103, 141, 153
Canoe River, 31
Carpenter, Eli, 60
Castlegar, British Columbia, 105, 131, 151
Celgar Company, 117
Christmas trees, 133
Church, Frank, 143
Churchill River, 23
Clark Fork River, 4, 28, 29, 32

161

Cleaver, John, 66
Coccola, Fr. Nicholas, *39*, 63, 65, 67
Columbia and Kootenay Steam Navigation Company, 93, 95
Columbia Lake, 27, 34, 75, 84, 91
Columbia River, 6, 24, 25, 27, 29-35, 37, 42, 75, 76, 80, 86, 91, 96, 123, 133, 136, 141, 143, 145, 151
Consolidated Mining and Smelting Company (Cominco), 57, 66, 67, 127
Corbin, Daniel C., 102
Cranbrook, British Columbia, 34, *95*, 113, 118; airport, 119; automobiles in, 123; founded, 74; railroad reaches, 98, 99; recent growth, 132; sawmills, 104
Cranbrook Lumber Company, 104
Crestbrook Forest Industries, 117
Creston, British Columbia, 7, 27, 117, 119, 123, 124, 129, 132, 136
Crows Nest Coal Company, 99
Crowsnest Lumber Company, 104, *114*
Crows Nest Pass, 46, 98, 123
Crowsnest Railway, *93*, *94*, 96-99, 102, 104

David, Chief of Kutenais, 44
Dawson Lumber Company, *110*, 111
Demers, Fr., 35
Depew, Harry, 86
DeSmet, Fr. Pierre Jean, 21, 35, *36*
Dewdney, Edgar, *51*-53
Dewdney Trail, 52, *53*
Deweyville, Montana, 99
Diefenbaker, John, 143
Donkey engine, *107*, 108
Dore, Robert, 45, 46
Doty, James, 37
Douglas, David, 33, *34*
Doukhobors, 131
Downey, Bart, 68

Dulles, John Foster, 139
Duncan Lake, 143, 145, 150
Dunlap, A.F., 72

East Kootenay Lumber Company, 104
East Kootenay River and Light Company, 137
Eastport, Idaho, 102
Edwards, Walter, 118
Eisenhower, Dwight D., 140, 143
Elk Mountain, 146
Elk River, *110*
Eureka Lumber Company, *111*, 113
Eureka Montana, 72, 99, *100*, 113, 124, 133, 150

Fairmont Hot Springs, 34
Fernie, British Columbia, 7, 91, *97*-99, 124
Fernie, Peter, 74
Fernie, William, *48*, 58, 98
Finlay, Jaco, 45
Finlay, Jacques Raphael "Jaco", 24
Fisher, Jack, 49
Fisher Creek, 72, 81, 126
Flat Bows, 7 (see also Kutenai Indians)
Flathead (Salish) Indians, 8, 28, 33, 35, 44
Flathead Lake, 29, 35
Flathead Reservation, 44, 53
Flathead Tunnel, *139*, *140*, 146, 148
Flowers, Tom, 103
Ford, Gerald, *149*, 153
Forest fire, 1910, 107
Forest reserves, 105-107
Fort Churchill, 23
Fort Colville, 42, 45
Fort Kootenai, 33, 34, 39, 41, 45, 46
Fort Shepherd, 53
Fort Steele, British Columbia, 7, 63, 66, *67*, 86, 89, 98, 99, 124, *126*
Fouquet, Fr. Leon, 37, *38*
French Charley, 68
Fry, Richard, 51, 53, 92

162

Galbraith, John, 51, 52
Galbraith, Robert, 51, 52
Galena, 87, 92
Gateway, Montana, 99
Georgia Pacific, 117
Glacial Lake Kootenai, 4
Glacial Lake Missoula, 4
Goat River, 53
Gold Creek, *110*
Golden, British Columbia, 84, 86, 102, 118
Granite Creek, 72, 126
Great National Parks Auto Highway, 120
Great Northern Railway, 68, 72, 81-84, *83*, 89, 92, 93, 95, 96, *98*, 99, 102, 104, 138, 146
Green, Howard, 142
Griffith, Dave, 45
Grohman, British Columbia, 77, 91, *104*
Gwendoline, 84, 86, 88, 89

Hall, E. O., 118-*120*
Hall brothers, 58, 59, 92
Hamilton, William, 43
Hammill, Thomas, *52*, 57
Haney, M. J., 96
Hanson, Nils, 120
Haskell, Charles R. B., 81
Haskell Pass, 81
Hearst, George, 57
Hector, James, 39, 41, *42*, 45
Heinze, F. Augustus, 63, 96, 99
Hendryx, W. A., 57
Herring, Joe, 49
Hewitt, Col. L. H., 136
Hill, James Jerome, 71-*81*, 96, 99
Horse Indians, 7 (see also Kutenai Indians)
Howse, Joseph, 24, *29*
Howse Pass, 24, 30, 32
Hoy, Capt. Ernest C., 118, *119*
Hudson's Bay Company, 23, 24, 29. 33, 34, 38, 46, 53
Hulse, Robert, 68

Ice Age, 3, 4
Idaho, 92
Industrial Workers of the World, 113

International, 90, 95
International Joint Commission, 137-142
International Molybdenum Co., 126
Isadore, Kutenai Chief, 63, 65
Isodore-Keith, Kutenai Chief, *13*
Itschner, Col. E. C., 137

J. D. Farrell, 85, 89
J. Neils Lumber Company, 113, *116*, 117, 139
Japanese relocation, 132
Jennings, Montana, 7, 28, 81, 84, 86, 89, 104, 113
Johnson, Lyndon B., 145, 148
Jones, B. Walter, 86, 88
Kaniksu National Forest, 106
Kapula, 63, 65
Kaslo, 90, 93
Kaslo, British Columbia, *60*, 92, 96, 105, 109, 132
Kelly, Edward, 57
Kennedy, Dan, 49
Kennedy, John F., 145
Kimberley, British Columbia, 99, 124, 127, 134
Kittson, William, 33
Kokanee, *91*, 95
Kootenae House, 25, 27, 28, 32
Kootenai, 93
Kootenai Canyon, 82
Kootenai Falls, *3*, 27, 28, 110, 135
Kootenai Mining and Smelting Company, 57, 92
Kootenai National Forest, 106, 133
Kootenai Pass, 41
Kootenai Power Construction Company, 134
Kootenai Railway and Navigation Company, 93
Kootenai River, abandonment of 1870's, 53; agriculture on, 72-75, 128, 129; airplanes, 118; automobiles, 118; Baillie-Grohman diversion canal on, 75, *76*, 77, *78*; bridges, *122*, 123, *126*, 146, 151; dams, *132-134*; David Douglas on, 33; David Thompson reaches, 27;

163

ferries, 50-52, 120; first inhabitants, 6; floods, 95, 129, 136; forest reserves, 105-107; Fort Steele established on, 63; fur trade on, 32; geological formation, 1-5; George Simpson on, 34, 35; gold discovery, 45; highways, 120, 123, 124; James Sinclair on, 38, 39; log drives on, 109-111; navigation by fur traders, 33; orchards, 72, 74, 128, 129; Palliser expeditions near, 39, 41-43; Pierre Jean DeSmet on, 35, 37; railroads to 79-84, 96-102; recent mining, 126, 127; reclamation, 129; second mining rush, 55-72; steamboats on, 84-96; tourist trade, 124; wood products industry, 103-117; see also Libby Dam

Kootenai River Transportation Company, 89

Kootenay Central Railway, 102

Kootenay Forest Products Ltd., 117

Kootenay Lake, 53, 123, 133, 150; agriculture on, 74, 75, 128-*130*; air harbors, 119, Baillie-Grohman and, 76-78; David Thompson on, 27; forest fire, 107; fruit boom, 128, 129, *130*; geological formation, 2; Indians on, 7; John Palliser on, 42; mining on, 55-60; Nelson founded on, 58, 59; railroads to, 92, 96-99; steamboats on, 91-96; tourist trade, 124; wood products industry, 105, 109, 117

Kootenay Landing, 96, 104

Kootenay National Park, 124, *125*

Kootenay Pass, 124

Killyspel House, 28

Kuskanook, British Columbia, 99

Kutenai Indians, 4, 7, 9, 11, 13, 16, *20*; agriculture, 12; canoes, 15, 16; ceremonies, 17; character, 21, 22; clothing, 13, 14; David Thompson meets, 27; fish festival, 11; fishing, 10; funerals, 19; fur trade, 33; horses, 15; housing, 14, 15, *20*; hunting, 8-10; language, 8; leisure activities, 18; marriage and family, 18, 19; meaning of name, 8; missionaries among, 35-37; origins, 6; painting, 8, 14; plant use by, 12; religion, 17; reservations, 44; Shaman, 17, 18; skirmish in Wild Horse, 63, 65; skirmish with Blackfeet, 43, 44; skirmish with Libby miners, 49; sweat lodge, 15; tools, 12, 13; tribal organization, 19, 21; utensils, 12; warfare, 18; weapons, 9

Lake Koocanusa, 5, 126, *146*, 151-*153*

Lake Pend Orielle, 28

Lawson, Jack, 47

Leitch, Archie, 104

LeRoi Mines, 60, 63

Lethbridge, Alberta, 96, 118

Lewis, Meriwether, 24

Libby, Montana, 2, 7, *69*, *70*, 86, 107, 124, 150; airport, 119; automobiles in, 120, *122*, 123; county seat, 72; fire department, *124*; founded, 68; gold discovery, 49; gold rush of 1880's, 68; mining near, 72, 126, 127; sawmills, 104, *110*, 113, 115-117; trading posts established near, 28, 33; see also Libby Dam

Libby Creek, 49, 67

Libby Dam, 5, 124, 135-154, *137*, *150*, *153*; authorized, 137; construction, *138*, *141*, 144, 147-152; dedication, *149*, 152, 153; design, 145-147; electric power from, 146, 151, 153; fish hatchery, 152; social problems, 148, 150, 152, 153;

164

U.S.-Canadian negotiations, 137-145
Lincoln County, Montana, 72, 113, 123, 126, 128, 133, 148, 150, 152
Linklater, John, 33, 39, 45
Livestock industry, 72, 73
Lumber and Sawmill Union, 115
Lumber and Timber Union, 115
Lumberton Sawmill, 113, *114*
Lund, Peter, 104
Lytton, 93

MacDonald, Donald, 153
McDonald, Finan, 24, 27, 28
McGillivray, William, 27
McGillivray's Portage, 27, 37, 75, 76
McGinty Trail, 66, 86
McKay, Alex, 43
McKenzie, Donald, 32
McMillan, James, 28
McNaughton, A. G. L., 138, 139, 141, 142
McTavish, John George, 32
Manning, James, 45
Mansfield, Mike, 137, 141, 143, 147
Marysville, British Columbia, 66
Mather, Robert, 74
Menetrey, Joseph, 37
Metcalf, Lee, 141, 143
Mica Creek, 143, 145
Mica Dam, 151
Michelle, Chief of Kutenais, 44
Midge, *87*, 91, 92
Montana Fish and Game Department, 152
Montour, Nicholas, 32
Morigeau, Francois, 37
Morrison-Knudsen Company, 148
Moyie, 92, 95, 96
Moyie Lake, 42, 67
Moyie River, 27, 34, 38, 113
Moyie Springs, 120
Moyie Valley, 3, 50
Mullan, Lt. John, 37
Murray, James E., 140

Nakusp, British Columbia, 92
Neils, Julius, 113
Nelson, *89*, 93
Nelson, British Columbia, *59*, 92, 96, 98, 118; automobiles, 120, *122*; early settlement, 59; founded, 58; opera house, 60, *61*; sawmills, 109, 117; tram, *61*
Nelson and Fort Shepherd Railway, 96
Nelson River, 23
Newgate, Montana, 99
Nixon, Richard M., 151
North Star, *85*, 88, 89, 91
North Star Mill, 104
North Star Mine, 65, 66, 84, 86
North West Company, 23, 24, 27-33
Northern Pacific Railway, 81, 91
Order of Oblates, 37
Oregon Treaty, 35
O'Reilly, Peter, 46, *47*, 48
Pacific Fur Company, 31
Pacific Western Airlines, 119
Palliser, Capt. John, 39, 41, *42*, 43
Payne Mine, 60
Pearson, Lester, 145
Pend D'Orielle Indians, 8, 44
Perry, Frank, 49
Peter Serelle and Co. Sawmill, *112*
Phillips, Michael, 46, 74, 103
Pierre, 67
Pillet, Francis Benjamin, 32
Pilot Bay, 57
Pipe Creek, 13, 110
Preston, E.L., 82
Proctor, British Columbia, 96, 98
Purcell Mountains, 1, 79
Purcell Trench, 2, 3

Rainy Creek, 126, 127
Rexford, Montana, 99, 123, *147*, 150
Robson, British Columbia, 96
Rocky Mountain House, 23, 24
Rocky Mountain Trench, 2, 3, 6, 79

165

Rocky Mountains, 1-3, 23, 41, 79, 118, 154
Rogers, Major A.B., *80*
Rossland, British Columbia, 63, *64*
Rustler, 86, 88
Ruth, 86, 88

St. Eugene Mine, 67
St. Eugene's Mission, 37, *40*, 63, 67, 96
St. Ignatius Mission, 35, 37
St. Mary's Mission, 35
St. Mary's River, 37
St. Regis Paper Company, 116, 117
Saleesh House, 28, 31
Salmon River, 42, 58
Sandon, British Columbia, 60, 62, *64*, 132
Sandpoint, Idaho, 92
Saskatchewan River, 23, 24
Sato, Bob, 152
Seaton, John, 60
Selkirk Mountains, 79, 105
Silver Crown Mine, 72
Silver King Mine, *56*, 58, 59
Simpson, Sir George, 34, 35, 38, *41*
Sinclair, James, 38, 39, *43*
Sinclair Pass, 123
Skookumchuk Pulp Mill, 117
Slocan District, 60, 96, 132
Slocan Lakes, 6, 60
Slocan Star Mine, 60
Smith, Ed, 66
Snake River, 32, 136
Snare Indians, 6
Snowshoe Mine, 72
Snowstorm Mine 72
Sons of Freedom, 131
Spokane, Washington, 55, 102
Spokane Falls and Northern Railway, 96
Spokane House, 31
Sproat, Gilbert Malcolm, 59, 79
Sproule, Robert E., 57
Stanley, A.O., 139
Stark, W.M., 118
State of Idaho, 88, 93
Steamboats, 84-96

Steele, Colonel Sam, 63, *65*
Stein Lumber Company, 109
Stevens, Isaac, 37, 44
Stevens, John F., 81
Stonechest, James, 68
Stoop, Frank, 120
Sullivan, John William, 21, 39, 41, 42, 53
Sullivan, Pat, 66
Sullivan Mine, 66, 99, 127, *128*, *129*, 134

Therriault, Charles, 103
Thompson, Charlotte Small, 23, 24
Thompson, David, 32, 35, 39, 75, 103; birth and early career, 23; death, 31; crosses Rocky Mountains, 24, 25; farming near Kootenai, 28; first attempt to cross Rocky Mountains, 24; founds Kootenae House, 26; founds Kullyspell House, 28; founds Saleesh House, 28; journal, *26*, 28; map, *25*, 31; meets Kutenai Indians, 27; memorial, *30*; reaches Columbia River, 24; reaches Kootenai River, 27; trip to mouth of Columbia, 31; winter on upper Columbia, 30
Tie hacks, 103
Toad Mountain, 58
Tobacco Plains, 7, 12, 28, 33, 37, 39, 45, 50, 66, 72, 99, 104, 111, 128
Trail, British Columbia, 63, 89, 96, 99, 127, 134
Trail Creek, 60, 63
Troy, Montana, 2, 68, 72, *83*, 107, 119, 120, 123; founded, 82; sawmills, 113, 116
Trudeau, Pierre, 152
Truman, Harry S., 137
Turney-High, H.H., 8

U.S. Army Corps of Engineers, 136-152
U.S. Forest Service, 146, 152

166

Upper Columbia Navigation and Tramway Company, 84, 86
Upper Kootenai Navigation Company, 86

Van Wyck, Henry, 68
Vermiculite, 126, *127*
Vermillion Pass, 34, 123
Vermillion River, 34, 68

W.R. Grace Company, *127*
Waldie and Sons Sawmill, 105
Walker, Thomas, 47
Walton, John, 51
Wardner, British Columbia, 104, 123
Warland, Montana, *100*, 113
Wegen, O.J., 74
West Kootenay Power and Light Company, 133, 134
Western News, 113, 126
Weyerhaeuser, Frederick, 109
Wilby, Thomas W., 123
Wild Horse Creek, *49*, 45-53, 57, 63, 79, 103
Windermere, British Columbia, 7, 44
Windermere Lake, 25
Wood products industry, 103-118; camp conditions, 108, 109; river drives, 109-111; strikes, 109, 113
Wood River, 30

Yaak River, 3, 72, 110, 120, 134
Yahk, British Columbia, 123
Yarnell Island, *5*
"Yeast Powder Bill", 47

Zonolite Company, 126, 139

167